City Breaks
in
Paris

REG BUTLER

In Association with

THOMSON HOLIDAYS

SETTLE PRESS

Text © 1989 Reg Butler
7th Edition 1997

First published by Settle Press
10 Boyne Terrace Mews
London W11 3LR

ISBN (Paperback) 1 872876 49 8

Printed by Villiers Publications
19 Sylvan Avenue
London N3 2LE

Foreword

As Britain's leading short breaks specialist, we recognise the need for detailed information and guidance for you, the would-be traveller. But much more is required than just a listing of museums and their opening times. For a few days, the CityBreak visitor wants to experience the local continental lifestyle.

We are therefore very pleased to work with Reg Butler and Settle Press on the CityBreak series of pocket guide-books. Reg Butler has provided a very readable book packed not only with important practical information but with colourful observations in a personal style that captures the very essence of your City Break destination.

As well as CityBreaks in Paris, other books in the series cover Rome, Florence and Venice; Amsterdam; Vienna, Salzburg, Budapest and Prague; Dublin; Brussels and Bruges; Madrid, Barcelona, Seville and Granada; New York, Boston and Washington. Thomson also operate to many other world cities from departure points across the UK.

We're sure you'll find this book invaluable in planning your short break in Paris.

In this revised edition, all opening hours, prices, phone numbers and restaurant recommendations have been checked by Thomson's resident staff and reps in Paris. Working there year-round, they have the huge advantage of being able to monitor changes as they happen. Inevitably, more changes will occur between the date of printing and when the reader travels. But this guide-book should still be the most up-to-date on the market!

THOMSON CITYBREAKS

Contents

MAPS

Chapter One

Paris is Always in Season

Paris is always in season, whatever the time of year. Starting from October, one of Europe's biggest Exhibitions, the Paris Motor Show attracts many extra visitors. Then around Christmas and New Year, there are regular visitors from all neighbouring countries, snatching a few days' break to bring the champagne sparkle into winter or to visit the 'Sales'.

Then it's springtime – and *everyone's* heard about the magic of Paris in the Spring. Easter – Whitsun – and it's summer traffic again...

Curiously, Paris is 'empty' in August, when the local citizens take off for a month's holiday, surrendering the capital to visitors from abroad. August city traffic is relatively light and jam-free. A car-driver can even find parking space. Many non-tourist shops close for the month.

Whatever the season, all the delights of Paris are awaiting: the pleasures of sightseeing, sitting at boulevard cafés or sampling the great museums; of dining out in colourful restaurants, and revelling in the night-life.

To keep food-and-drink expenses under control, pack a knife and a corkscrew. Central Paris is full of delightful picnic spots alongside the Seine or in the parks. There's no hardship in lunching off a bottle of wine, French loaf, cheese, ham and salad. On a warm day, that kind of lunch can be sheer delight – much more the flavour of Paris than hunting around for a fast-food hamburger franchise. There are hundreds of restaurants that offer a good fixed-price menu, with all details posted outside the doorway. Watch for establishments that are crowded

7

with Parisians shortly after noontime. The locals know best!

To get your bearings, take a city-sightseeing tour by coach. Some tours cover most of the sights in half a day. You can then work out which areas you want to re-visit in more detail; or which museums and galleries you'd like to tackle.

Chapter Five of this guidebook is headed 'Star highlights – not to be missed'. But don't get yourself fully programmed, morning till night. If you're ticking off a long list of things you want to see, just accept that you probably won't manage to work through them all. Leave some for next time!

It's counter-productive to turn Paris into an asssult course. You're in the French capital to enjoy yourself, to get its flavour and enjoy the unexpected. Many pleasures come to the visitor without advance planning. Make time to saunter around, letting each sight capture your attention until another distraction catches your eye.

Refreshment at a pavement café is much more than just a way of quenching thirst or giving your ankles a rest. It's an essential part of the Parisian life-style, enjoying a ringside seat to all the street happenings.

Excursions? For an hour or so, take a Bateaux Mouches boat trip along the Seine; or, one evening, spoil yourself with a luxury-grade dinner cruise to the sound of soft music. For a half-day excursion, Versailles Palace is first choice. If the weather is good, travel out to Fontainebleau, set amid the most beautiful woodlands of France.

It's a popular idea that Paris means Romance. Champagne and flowers can easily be arranged to await your arrival at the chosen hotel. Romance isn't just for newly-weds, or couples who are thinking about it. A similar deal can help set the mood for anyone celebrating a silver, gold, ruby or diamond anniversary – much better than spending the money on something sensible like a new tumble dryer.

In fact, to start the trip in truly memorable style, why not go by Orient Express from Victoria, wallowing in 19th-century nostalgia? Here's how the Victorians and Edwardians departed on their Parisian idylls that gave France its champagne-and-oysters reputation.

Mention of Paris normally sparkles the imagination of potential visitors, both male and female. Men may be thinking of nightlife, while the girls probably have shopping in mind.

Both these pursuits can be costly, depending more precisely what you have in mind.

Night-life is the most dazzling in Europe, from big-time spectacular theatre shows like the Lido, down to off-beat cabaret in dubious clip-joints. If you sample a different cabaret show every night, the supply will hold out for a year.

For a seat close to the stage in top-flight shows like the Lido or the Paradis Latin – where the girls are dressed in ostrich plumes and French perfume – you must book the all-inclusive deluxe dinner arrangement. There are endless variations on Paris by Night packages. The big advantage is knowing precisely what the evening will cost. Go-it-alone you can have fun, but then be shattered when the final bill is presented.

So much to see – so much to do – the likelihood is that Paris will draw you back. City breaks in Paris never seem to last long enough.

Chapter Two

Your Arrival and Hotel

Arriving by train

By Eurostar, arrival is at Gare du Nord, which offers easy connections by Métro or taxi to your hotel. Incidentally, on departure home, the train ticket must be machine-stamped by the passenger, to validate the ticket with time and date.

By the luxury-style Orient Express, arrival or departure is at Gare de l'Est.

Arriving by air

From Charles de Gaulle airport (located north of Paris), there are several options:

- Air France coaches, every 12 minutes, for a 35-minute journey to Etoile, which has good Métro connections; or coaches every hour or half-hour to Montparnasse. Fares are 55F or 65F respectively.
- Frequent RER express-subway trains to Gare du Nord for a 35-minute journey. Cost 67F in 1st class, 45F in 2nd class.
- By taxi, costing over 190F to central Paris.

From Orly airport (located south of Paris):

- Air France coaches to Invalides air terminal and Montparnasse station. Fare 40F.
- A combined ticket covering shuttle service for the train going to Gare d'Austerlitz, plus Métro, costing 42.50F 1st class, or 28F 2nd class.

Self Drive

From the Dover-Calais ferry, or from Le Shuttle's Folkestone-Calais terminal, follow signs for the N1 motorway to Paris.

At your hotel

Breakfast - You will be charged extra at most hotels if you require more than the basic Continental breakfast. You may find it preferable to go to a nearby café if breakfast matters much to you.

Drinks and Minibars – Minibars are becoming more common in higher graded hotels, but check prices as the drinks may be expensive. Hotels without bars often have a drinks machine, or may sell soft drinks from reception.

Getting in Late – If you arrive back late at night, or in the early hours, and find the hotel door shut, just ring the bell (*sonnerie*) for the night porter (*veilleur de nuit*). Remember that other hotel guests may be asleep when you return.

Hotel corridors sometimes have a time switch for the lights to allow you enough time to unlock your door. Look for a small orange light and press the button.

In hotel WCs – and also in restaurants, etc. – you will not always find a light switch, as it may operate only when you lock the door.

Electric voltage – Voltage is 220V (suitable for UK 240V appliances). Plugs are the standard European two-pin round. Pack a plug adaptor for any equipment you may wish to use.

Tipping – Service is added to the bill (shown by the letters 's.t.c.' – service and taxes included). There is therefore no need to leave a gratuity.

Nevertheless it is customary to leave a small tip for the chambermaid – say 15 or 20F for a three or four day stay, more if you stay a week (say 25-30F). If the concierge or any other staff have been specially helpful (getting taxis, making telephone enquiries, etc.), they should be given something.

In general, tip to show appreciation for a special service (see chapter twelve on tipping in general).

Safety Deposit Boxes are available at most hotels.

Day of Departure – You must vacate your room by midday on the day of your departure. The Paris hotel day begins and ends strictly at midday. The hotel will usually look after your luggage until the time you need to collect it. But if space is difficult don't make unreasonable demands.

Chapter Three

Getting around Paris

3.1 The city layout

Paris is an easy city to find your way around. The river Seine flows east to west. North of the river is the Right Bank (*Rive Droite*). South of the river is the Left Bank (*Rive Gauche*).

Certain landmarks you will see repeatedly as you move around Paris. The Eiffel Tower is to the west. Montparnasse Tower is to the south, and central in relation to east and west. Montmartre and the white domes of Sacre-Coeur are to the north, central. Notre-Dame Cathedral is to the east in the heart of historic Paris.

The Arrondissement System

The key to finding any location in Paris is the arrondissement system. Arrondissements are districts and Paris is divided into twenty of them. They are arranged in a spiral of three (or more strictly 2½) circular segments going clockwise from the centre.

The centre segment consists of the arrondissements numbered 1 to 7. This is the heart of medieval Paris. The clockwise spiral starts with the first arrondissement which is approximately centred on the Louvre. For ease of reference, the Louvre may be regarded as the centre of Paris. The 8th arrondissement features the Champs Elysées.

The numbers of arrondissements are written as follows: 1er is the number for *Premier*, the 1st arrondissement; 2e is the number for *Deuxième*, the 2nd; etc. The numbers of arrondissements are thus indicated in this guidebook.

Key to Orientation Map of Paris

Key nos.

Arc de Triomphe, 8e	1
Army Museum, 7e	6
Carrousel Arch, 1er	17
Conciergerie, 1er	21
Ecole Militaire, 7e	5
Etoile, 8e	1
Galeries Lafayette, 9e	13
Grand Palais, 8e	8
Grévin Wax Museum, Montmartre, 9e	31
Grévin Museum, Forum des Halles, 1er	29
Hôtel de Ville – City Hall, 4e	23
Invalides, 7e	6
Louvre Museum, 1er	18
Luxembourg Gardens, 6e	19
Madeleine Church, 8e	12
Modern Art Museum, Pompidou Centre, 4e	30
Monmartre Cemetery, 18e	33
Musée d'Orsay, 7e	16
National Assembly, 7e	10
Notre Dame cathedral, 4e	22
Obelisque - Place de la Concorde, 8e	11
Opera House - Garnier, 9e	14
Opera House - Bastille, 12e	25
Orangerie Museum, Tuileries, 1er	15
Palais de la Découverte, 8e	6
Palais de Chaillot, 16e	2
Petit Palais, 8e	9
Picasso Museum, 3e	27
Place du Tertre, 18e	34
Place Pigalle, 18e	32
Place des Vosges, the Marais, 4e	26
Pompidou Centre, 4e	30
Printemps Department Store, 9e	13
Rodin Museum, 7e	7
Sacré-Coeur Basilica, 18e	34
Sainte-Chapelle, 1er	21
Samaritaine Department Store, 1er	28
Sewers of Paris, 7e	4
Sorbonne, 5e	20
Tour St Jacques, 4e	24

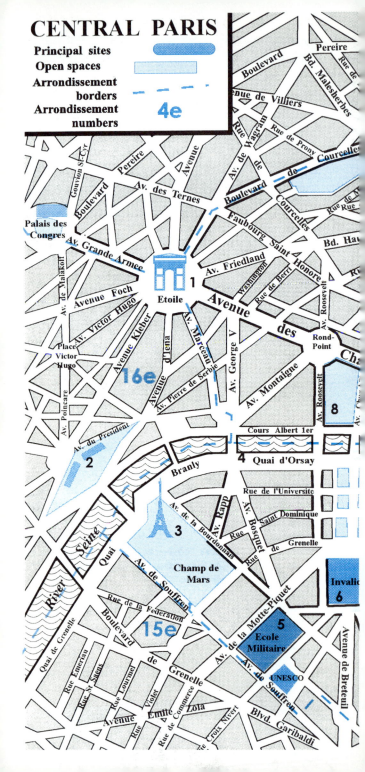

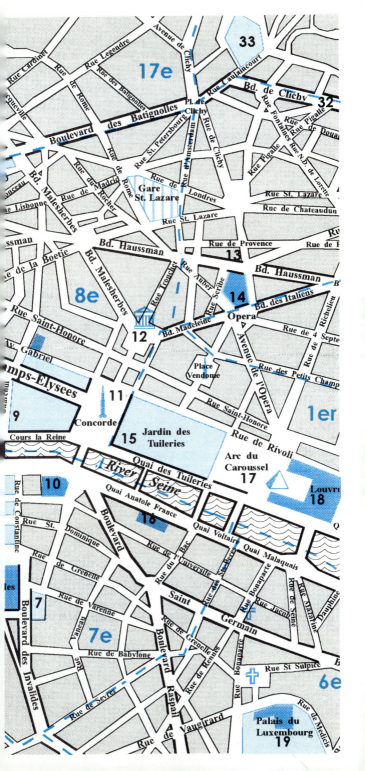

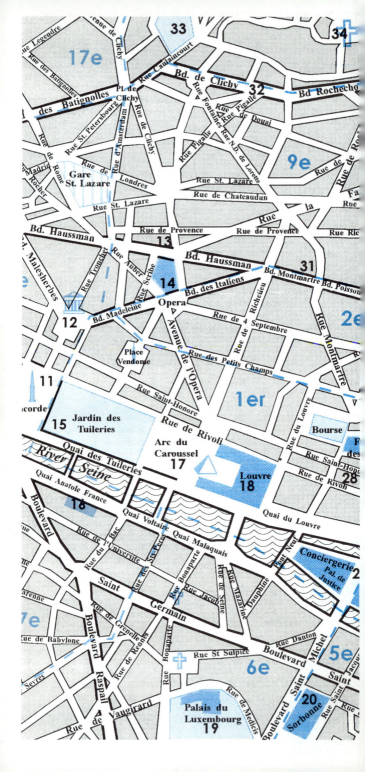

3.2 Public Transport

Paris has an outstanding public transport system. Its underground train service (Métro) is the best in the world. But don't ignore buses which can often prove a more interesting method of travel. A third element in the system is an urban express railway called RER.

Tickets

The same tickets are valid for the Métro and for buses (and also for RER within the city limits).

You can buy tickets singly, at 8F each. But it is much cheaper to buy them in booklets of 10, called *carnets*, costing 46F. These can be bought from Métro booking halls and at tobacco shops.

For longer-stay visitors, best value is the *Carte Orange* (or Orange Pass) which enables you to buy a weekly season ticket (from Monday to Sunday) called a 'Coupon Jaune', or a monthly season ticket.

More convenient for short-stay tourists, but comparatively expensive, is the Tourist Pass – the Billet de Tourisme. This can be bought from larger Métro stations and mainline railway stations on production of a passport. It is valid from whichever day you choose for either 2, 3 or 5 days. It gives you unlimited travel within Paris on buses, Métro and RER, plus discounts on some tourist attractions.

Costs of the *Paris Visite* Tourist Pass are 80F for 2 days; 110F for 3 days; 170F for 5 days. A one-day pass costs 50F.

Métro – Using the System

A Métro map can be obtained from any Métro station. Trains run from 05.30 hrs to 01.15 hrs (don't leave your last connection later than 0.30 hrs). The one-price ticket takes you everywhere on the Métro system.

To find your route, proceed as follows:

● Locate the name of the Métro station from which your journey is starting. Locate your destination and trace the route between the two stations.

● The Métro lines do not have names as in London. Instead you travel in the direction of the name of the station at the very end of the line. Thus, if you want to get from Charles de Gaulle-Etoile to Châtelet, you would look for signs saying 'Direction Château de Vincennes'.

● If you need to change lines you repeat the procedure. Thus, from Tuileries to Opéra you would travel to Palais Royal following the platform signs 'Château de Vincennes' and then to Opéra following the signs 'La Courneuve'. The French for 'interchange' or 'connection' is *correspondance*.

Buses

One ticket covers most journeys across central Paris. But buses differ from the Métro in that you may have to use two tickets for longer journeys.

Bus stops have their names displayed above them; this is also the name of the immediate area. A clear plan of the bus route is shown inside buses and at bus stops. This means that travelling by bus you can easily keep track of where you are.

On boarding, push your ticket into the machine for punching. If you have a pass – Coupon Jaune, Coupon Orange, or Billet de Tourisme – show it to the driver. Single tickets can be bought on the bus.

RER (Express Métro)

This is a rapid way of crossing Paris. There are four RER lines. They are best for longer journeys to suburbs and beyond.

There are interchanges between some RER stations and Métro stations. Normal Métro tickets can be used in the central fare stage. You may need to insert your used ticket into a machine to pass through the barriers when changing to Métro or vice-versa.

Taxis

Taxis are not expensive and you need not hesitate to use them in central Paris.

Only taxis displaying the illuminated sign 'Taxi Parisien' are registered taxis. Any other vehicle is not a taxi and may try to charge you an extortionate rate. A meter on the dashboard shows the fare and

the rate in use – A, B, or C. The rate increases for
night and for out-of-Paris areas. Additional charges
are made for baggage and for pick-ups from stations
and airports. Most drivers will not take more than
three passengers.

3.3 Sightseeing

If you can spare the time, the best way to get around
Paris is on foot. Paris is a pleasant and rewarding
city for walkers. When crossing roads, however,
even at pedestrian crossings, allow for the erratic
behaviour of Paris drivers. They have much less
consideration than in Britain or USA.

River Trips

The glass-roofed sightseeing boats are generally re-
ferred to as Bateaux Mouches. A Seine river trip is
a classic aspect of Paris sightseeing. Boats leave from
the right bank (north side) of the Pont de l'Alma, 8e.
Boats also operate from Pont-Neuf. Cost: 45F.

Coach Excursions Outside Paris

There are a number of excursions to a wide variety
of places within a day or half-day trip of Paris.
These excursions provide a guided tour in English.
The places include: Versailles, Chartres, Giverny
(home of Monet), Fontainebleau, and the Loire Val-
ley. See more details in Chapter 7.

Museum Pass

Buy a 'Carte Musée' which gives big savings and
unlimited entry to over 60 of the most famous museums and monuments in Paris, and avoiding the need
to queue.
Cost: 70F for one day; 140F for three days; 200F
for five days. Available from Métro stations and
museums, and from Thomson travel shop.

Paristoric - 11 bis Rue Scribe, 9e

An audiovisual extravaganza flashes through 2,000
years of Paris history in 45 minutes – setting the
cultural scene and background for your City Break.
On the hour, every hour. Cost 50F.   **Métro:** Opéra

Chapter Four
The great areas

Ile de la Cité

Shaped like a long canal-barge, the Ile de la Cité is one of the two islands that split the Seine. The original Parisii tribe converted this easy river crossing-point into a stronghold, but they couldn't hold out against Caesar. Their island town was burned by the Romans in 52 BC. The Roman settlers then built a Palace at the sharp end, and a temple at the other.

Centuries later, the Palace was still good enough to house the early kings of France. The site then became the seat of Parliament in the 14th century. Since the Revolution, the buildings were converted to Law Courts – the present-day Palais de Justice. The Conciergerie – north corner of the Palais de Justice – is the sombre jail where over 2500 condemned prisoners awaited transport to the guillotine during the French Revolution. Among them was Marie-Antoinette.

Facing the Law is the Church: Notre Dame (see Chapter 5). Climb the north and south towers, up there among the gargoyles, for that fantastic view made familiar by Victor Hugo's *Hunchback of Notre Dame*. Look down at the central bridges – Pont Notre Dame and Pont St. Michel – which stand where the Parisii settlers built their original wooden bridges to cross the Seine. Just imagine all the comings and goings, across 2000 years of history!

Walk all round the island embankments, looking every direction for a different view. Cross to the *quais* on the 'mainland', and get more pictures of Notre Dame. Browse among the bookstalls which also sell prints, postcards and general knick-knacks. The entire area is delightful!

Ile Saint-Louis

This is the second of the two boat-shaped islands, 'towed' by the Ile de la Cité, with a small bridge linking the two islands. The atmosphere is quite different: very peaceful, hard to imagine you're in the heart of a big city.

Most of the charming town houses were built 17th century. Peep into some of the courtyards. Wall plaques remind you of numerous artists, writers and politicians who made Ile Saint-Louis their home: people like Voltaire, Baudelaire, Cézanne.

Walk right round the *quais*, but also turn into the main street called Rue St.-Louis en l'Ile, with interesting shops including Berthillon's ice-cream parlour at no. 31. (See Chapter 15).

The Louvre and Rue de Rivoli

Start at Place de la Concorde (see Chapter 5) and stroll through the Tuileries gardens – formal and elegant, with statues everywhere. It's a good spot for a park-bench picnic, if there's room among the mothers and children.

Straight ahead is the Arc de Triomphe du Carrousel, built to celebrate Napoleon's 1805 crop of victories, a vintage year. Beyond is the Louvre. Look back, and you have a dead-straight line through to the Arc de Triomphe: the historic pomp-and-ceremony route.

One side of the Tuileries is the Seine. On the other side are the urbane shop colonnades of Rue de Rivoli, all designed in early 19th century. Stop for a photograph of Joan of Arc, golden on a horse, in the Place des Pyramides.

Saint-Honoré and the 8th arrondissement

This area stretches from Etoile (the huge traffic circle around the Arc de Triomphe), eastwards to Place de la Madeleine. It's a good address, with the President of France living in the Palais de l'Elysée, and the UK and US Embassies as close neighbours.

Along the Rue du Faubourg St.-Honoré, which runs parallel to the Champs-Elysées, shops offer luxury and opulence. It's an experience just to look at the very up-market window displays.

The Opéra Quarter

The Opera itself is among the world's great theatres. Around it swirls the traffic on one of the busiest intersections in Paris. Most famous of the café terraces is the Café de la Paix, where thousands of well-heeled tourists write their postcards.

Today it's mostly a business district all around, but with plentiful choice of cafés that serve good snacks. It's worth pausing in this area for a light self-service lunch.

Montmartre

In popular imagination, Montmartre became the spirit of Paris. Here were the brilliant artists, the lively women, the cabaret shows and nightlife, the picturesque streets, the zest and the passions and the laughter played out in a captivating setting.

Montmartre is situated on a hill to the north of the centre of Paris: at 423 feet this is the highest point of Paris. It is known as La Butte de Montmartre – *butte* meaning hillock – and Montmartre is often just called La Butte.

Montmartre was not incorporated into the city until 1860. It has retained a small-town look and also some of the flavour, with winding cobbled streets, charming little squares and the only vineyard in Paris.

The heyday of Montmartre was around the turn of the century, when the painter Toulouse-Lautrec frequented the Moulin Rouge and personalities like Zola, Degas, Renoir and Van Gogh lived in the area. Its legendary time is past. But the old village is still beautiful, and the area very much alive.

Montmartre has strikingly different aspects to its character. At the foot of the hill is the red light district, around the Place Pigalle and the Boulevard de Clichy. This is also the centre of cabarets and strip shows where the Moulin Rouge is still going strong as a reminder of past glories.

The paramount sight of Montmartre is the church of Sacré-Coeur (see separate entry, chapter five). The heart of the old village for tourist purposes is Place du Tertre – very photogenic, still picturesque and replete with café terraces, artists and easels, and musicians.

23

Note that you can use a Métro ticket on the funicular railway which takes you most way up the hill. If you walk up the Rue Foyatier, you climb 225 steps.

Most people approach from this direction below Sacré-Coeur (**Métro:** Anvers). An alternative is to take the Métro either to Lamarck-Coulaincourt or Abbesses stations. From there it is fun to wander through the little streets of the village before coming to Sacré-Cocur itself.

Métro: Anvers/Abbesses/Pigalle/Blanche/Lamarck-Caulaincourt.

Les Halles and the Beaubourg

Here, for 850 years, was 'the belly of Paris' – the food market which was exiled in 1979 to a ncw location near Orly airport. In its place is the Forum des Halles and the controversial Centre Pompidou, otherwise known as Beaubourg. The area has been re-born: the Forum is mostly an underground shopping complex, while the streets around are lively with bars and fast-food, and funky clothing stores.

The Pompidou Centre rates high among the world's most audacious buildings, arousing extreme outrage or admiration. There's nothing like it, anywhere in Europe. Go see for yourself! It's now the top tourist attraction in Paris, leaving the Eiffel Tower cold. (More details, see Chapter 5). South towards Place du Châtelet, there are numerous late-night jazz bars.

The Marais 3e and 4e

The Marais quarter is the oldest area in Paris and provides an intriguing and dramatic contrast to the rest of Paris.

It has survived by luck and good fortune. In the middle of the nineteenth century Paris was replanned and rebuilt under the direction of Baron Haussmann. Haussmann's boulevards surround the Marais district, but the Marais escaped being pulled down.

Its streets and buildings are substantially preserved from the Paris of the early seventeenth century. The heart of the Marais quarter is 300 acres of townscape now protected by preservation orders.

The Marais extends approximately from the Bastille in the east to the Rue de Temple and the Church of St Gervais in the west, and from the quays on the Seine to the Rue Pastourelle to the north.

To appreciate the district, just wander around the narrow twisting streets. Survey the architecture. Look at the grand mansions and their courtyards, examine the ancient buildings and the carvings above the windows.

In the seventeenth century this area was the height of fashion. Some of the stately mansions from that time are open to the public (the French word *hôtel* in this context means town mansion or large house).

It's preferable to visit the area on a weekday when access is more feasible. Located near the centre is the Place des Vosges – see Chapter 15.

Today, the pleasure of the area is not just as a museum piece of townscape. It has all the life and charm of today's Paris, with interesting shops and cafés around unexpected corners: a delightful and wholly successful blend of past and present.

Métro: Hotel-de-Ville/St-Paul/Chemin-Vert/St-Sébastian Froissart/Filles du Calvaire/Temple/Arts-et-Métiers.

The Latin Quarter

Just south of the river from the Palais de Justice and Notre Dame is the Quartier Latin, with cosmopolitan student life based on the Sorbonne – the world's second oldest university after Bologna. It's called Latin Quarter because – until the French Revolution – all teaching was in Medieval Latin, which served like Esperanto for intercourse between different nationalities.

For eight centuries the intellectual and bohemian life-style has flourished. Main street – an ex-Roman road – is Boulevard St-Michel, lined with bookstores and cafés. If you want to be real French, call it Boul'Mich. Here were the big student riots of May 1968. But the area has long since calmed down, particularly since decentralization of the student campuses.

The quarter is still home territory for young people of all nationalities. There are any number of cheap and lively ethnic restaurants and cafés. Vibrant activity continues late into the night, with small cinemas, discos, jazz cellars and clubs.

Saint-Germain-des-Prés, 6e

If you have time to include only one area of the Left Bank, the choice must fall between the Latin Quarter (5th arrondissement) in the east, and the area of St-Germain-des-Prés (6th arrondissement) further west.

For some people – especially the young – the Latin Quarter has the edge. It's an exhilarating focal point for the younger generation; has a colourful look from some of its winding medieval side streets; and there's lively activity at all times of day and night.

But we must give the St-Germain-des-Prés quarter precedence. It has the Left Bank atmosphere, coupled with Parisian excellence. If you have time to walk around at leisure, here in the eyes of many people is the most attractive area in Paris.

The area lies roughly between the Luxembourg Gardens and the Seine. The church of St-Germain-des-Prés is at its centre. The most distinguished part of the district is bounded approximately by Boulevard St-Germain and the river, and Rue des Saints-Pères to the west and Rue de Seine to the east.

Rue Bonaparte and Rue Jacob in particular are streets worth walking if only for the distinction of the shops. This area is rich in antique shops and galleries, chic dress shops and rare specialist shops. The houses are 17th and 18th century – look into the courtyards and side streets.

There are also interesting old streets and buildings south of Boulevard St-Germain, and the great church of St-Sulpice.

On Boulevard St-Germain, within yards of each other, are perhaps the three best known cafés in the Western world (Café de Flore, Deux Magots, and Lipp). The area is dotted with excellent cafés and restaurants that are lesser known, but with a wider range of prices.

Métro: St-Germain-des-Prés/Rue du Bac/Mabillon.

Montparnasse

On the Left Bank south of St-Germain, Montparnasse was formerly a brilliant international centre of art and bohemian life. Much of that intellectual sparkle now rests in Montparnasse Cemetery, where pilgrims can find the graves of Maupassant, Saint-Saens, Jean-Paul Sartre, Baudelaire and César Franck. A few cafés still manage to keep something of the old atmosphere, but today's writers and the expatriates have found other havens.

Champs-de-Mars and Trocadéro

Just to prove you've been in Paris, why not scoop the world and photograph the Eiffel Tower? Start from the Champ de Mars, an 18th-century parade ground, now a pleasant park where the Tower spreads its legs. All kinds of pictures present themselves – looking straight up, sideways, or however you like to tilt the camera. For human interest, weekends and Wednesdays the park features puppet-show performances at 3.15 and 4.15 p.m.

Cross the bridge – Pont d'Iéna – and try a different angle, with Eiffel Tower framed by trees along the quayside. Then climb up to the Palais de Chaillot, where tour coaches stop on the Place du Trocadéro to a waiting swarm of North African vendors selling souvenirs. From the terrace piazza you get the best Eiffel shots, with foreground statuary.

Chapter Five

Star highlights

5.1 Not to be missed

To enjoy the full flavour of Paris, here is a selection of top priority sites: monuments, city highlights and museums. Prices and seasonal opening times are liable to change, with shorter hours off-peak.

Arc de Triomphe, 8e – Place Charles de Gaulle

This famous landmark commemorates Napoleon's victories and has been a symbol of French national glory. The Tomb of the Unknown Soldier lies beneath and commemorates the dead of the two World Wars. There is a small museum inside. The rooftop offers a superb view of Paris. Open: 10.00-22.30 hrs; Sun-Mon 10-18 hrs. Cost 40F by lift or stairs.

Métro: Etoile

Champs-Elysées, 8e

A walk along the most famous avenue in Europe is a requirement for any visitor. It runs over a mile long from the Arc de Triomphe to the Place de la Concorde. There are two distinct halves of this great avenue. The division occurs at the traffic island called Rond Point.   **Métro:** Fr. D. Roosevelt

On the Place de la Concorde side of the Rond Point the avenue is flanked by gardens. West of the Rond Point the magnificent avenue rises gently to the Arc de Triomphe and it glitters with fashionable cafés and their pavement terraces, luxurious shops, and cinemas. Wide pavements lined with chestnut trees make it a boulevardier's domain.

The Avenue has suffered greatly from commercialisation. But its scale, and the lively human activity and shopping precincts are worth experiencing, though prices are high. The Champs-Elysées also provides a splendid setting for Paris by night, with street lamps shining on a lighted river of traffic.

Métro: Etoile/George V/Franklin D. Roosevelt/ Champs-Elysées Clemenceau/Concorde.

Place de la Concorde, 8e

This vast square was originally laid out in 1755 around an equestrian statue of Louis XV. The royal statue was pulled down during the French Revolution and replaced by the guillotine, which severed the heads of Louis XV1, Marie Antoinette, Danton, Robespierre and over 1300 others.

In 1795 the square was renamed 'Concorde'. The pink granite obelisk came from the temple of Rameses II at Thebes in upper Egypt (dated 1300 BC) and was erected in 1836 close to where the guillotine had stood. The fountains were created at the same time. The marble statues of rearing horses came from Louis XIV's palace at Marly.

West of the square is a view of the Champs-Elysées up to the Arc de Triomphe. In the opposite direction the view extends to the Louvre.

The square should also be seen at night, when lit by 600 lamps and spotlights. With the Champs-Elysées beyond, here is 'The City of Light'.

Métro: Concorde

Eiffel Tower, 7e

This world famous structure was built for the Universal Exhibition of 1889, designed as a symbol of the triumph of industrial civilisation and for decades later the tallest in the world. You can take lifts to each of the three stages and there are cafés on the first two. The lure of the Eiffel Tower is strong and the view is well worth the effort.

A memorable option is to have the set lunch at the Jules Verne restaurant on the second stage. It costs about £22.   Tel: 01 45 55 61 44. Open: 09.30-23.00 hrs daily; and from 09 hrs in summer. Cost: 1st Floor 20F; 2nd, 40F; top, 56F.

Métro: Champ de Mars/Trocadéro/Bir-Hakeim

Notre Dame Cathedral, 4e – Ile de la Cité

The cathedral of Paris is very much the city's church. This magnificent building is a masterpiece of Gothic harmony. It was built between the 12th and 14th centuries, though most of the sculptures on the facade are 19th century restorations.

The cathedral is nearly always crowded, but it's not too difficult to take in the main features of the interior. A good overall view is obtained from beneath the great organ at the west end of the nave.

For the exterior, besides the view of the west front across the square, go to the gardens on the east and south side, offering a clear view of the flying buttresses, the spire and the apse. For a view from the towers, see Chapter 15.

Open: 8-19 hrs.   **Métro:** Cité

Sacré-Coeur (Basilica), 18e
Rue du Chevalier-de-la-Barre, Montmartre

This church occupies a dramatic setting on the hill of Montmartre (the Butte), with a commanding view over Paris. Its gleaming white facade with beehive-like domes are known from countless travel pictures.

For maximum impact, you should approach it from the long flight of steps to the south. A funicular railway can take you part of the way uphill.

Sacré-Coeur was built by the Catholic church of Paris as a symbol of penitence for the acts of the Paris Commune in 1871, in the wake of the disastrous Franco-Prussian war.

A favourite view of Paris is from its steps (see Chapter 15). The dome is open daily from 06.45-23.00 hrs. A visit to the basilica could be combined with an exploration of Montmartre (see Chapter 4).

Métro: Anvers/Abbesses/Lamarck-Caulaincourt

La Sainte Chapelle, 1er
Boulevard du Palais, l'Ile de la Cité

This chapel has the most glorious and spellbinding stained-glass windows, and the whole chapel conveys a sense of beauty and lightness and transcendence beyond description. The Sainte Chapelle is in fact two chapels. There is a Lower Chapel from which you reach the Upper Chapel by way of narrow, winding stairs. It is the soaring Upper Chapel that is the incomparable masterpiece. It was built in the thirteenth century and the stained glass is the oldest remaining in Paris.

Except for the spire topped with a crown of thorns, the Sainte Chapelle is concealed from the outside world, hidden in the precincts of the Palais de Justice.

Open 10–17 or 18 hrs. Entrance 32F, Students and Seniors 21F. Also visit the Conciergerie, where Marie Antionette was imprisoned.   **Métro:** Cité

Galeries Lafayette Department Store, 9e
Printemps Department Store, 9e
Boulevard Haussmann

No new visitor to Paris should overlook these two great department stores which stand next to each other. The stores are located just behind the Opera House.

Built early this century, the buildings still astonish by their daring. Their exuberant and elegant design is wholly right for their purpose. At street level, they are alight with brilliant window dressing. The quality of the interior decor and ornament is also outstanding.

Of special appeal is the Belle Epoque style of the Au Printemps tea salon beneath a stained-glass rotunda (sixth floor); and in Galeries Lafayette the superb glass and steel dome.

Many claim that Galeries Lafayette is the best department store in the world. Both it and Printemps are unsurpassed. They have unerring style combined with playfulness. They emanate a very Parisian excitement and élan.

The two stores offer a quick survey of the newest and brightest in the Paris shopping scene, whether in fashion, furniture or household wares. For more details, see Chapter 8 on Shopping.

Métro: Chausée d'Antin/Opéra/Havre-Caumartin

The Invalides, 7e

The Hôtel des Invalides was built by Louis XIV in the 1670's as a home for wounded war veterans. It is the largest and possibly the greatest monumental group of buildings in Paris.

HIGHLIGHTS

The most inspired element is the Church of the Dome, a Parisian landmark. The building is regarded as one of the best examples of French classical architecture. It is, however, more visited for the tomb of Napoleon Bonaparte, whose body was brought to this grandiose resting place from St Helena in 1840.

Les Invalides now houses three museums. The Army Museum (Musée de l'Armée) is among the best of its kind, with perhaps the world's largest collection of arms from the medieval period onwards. (See Museums, Chapter 6).

Another museum relates to the two World Wars, while the third collection is devoted to the French Resistance during World War II.

Les Invalides is classical Paris in its full glory. The long facade (645 feet) is among the finest in Paris and looks onto a majestic esplanade stretching down to the Seine. For the fullest effect and an overall view, you should approach the Invalides from the Alexandre III Bridge.

Open: 10-17 or 18 hrs. Cost: 35F (reduced 25F).
Métro: Invalides/Latour-Maubourg/Varenne/Ecole-Militaire.

5.2 *The great museums*

On a short stay it may be impossible to visit each of the major art museums highlighted in this chapter. One can only pick out those of greatest appeal.

Art collections are spread out as follows among the big three national museums:

- The Louvre up to the early 19th century.
- Musée d'Orsay for 19th and early 20th centuries.
- The Pompidou Centre's Museum of Modern Art for 20th century.

These museums are described in this chapter together with the Museum of Science, Technology and Industry at the Villette Park on the city outskirts.

While you should try to see at least one of these major museums during your stay, also remember that Paris has a wealth of other smaller museums which can be enjoyed. For instance, as an alternative to the Impressionists at the Musée d'Orsay, you can see some incomparable Monets and other Impressionists in the Musée Marmottan housed in the quiet of the 16th arrondissement. Or you can see a collection of great Impressionist paintings at the Orangerie – two minutes from the Louvre – where the pictures are more easily absorbed than in a larger museum, and in more pleasurable conditions.

Likewise, if you cannot take your children to the Science City at La Villette, they can see live scientific demonstrations at the Musée-Palais de la Découverte (Palace of Discovery) in Avenue Franklin Roosevelt (8e).

The smaller Paris museums certainly cover an extensive and unusual range of interests, including such gems as the Cluny museum, Hôtel Biron (Rodin Museum), Guimet Museum, Picasso Museum, Victor Hugo House, and Hôtel Carnavalet.

Finally, a reminder: consider buying a Museum Pass – details at end of Chapter 3.

The Louvre, 1er

The Louvre has the greatest collection of fine art of any museum in the world. In particular, it is supreme in its collection of paintings. Its size is overwhelming. There are over 200 different galleries, the largest much longer than a football pitch. What do you do about seeing it?

Here are some suggestions for newcomers.

First, you can admire it from the outside, for the Louvre is a former royal palace in a magnificent setting. The present vast building has grown over the centuries from the Renaissance onwards, and would be worth a good look even if it were empty inside.

Realise that it's impossible to visit more than a very small sample of the museum. Restrict your ambitions. If there is a part of the collections which particularly interest you, study a plan of the museum and select and see a manageable number of galleries. A good choice of catalogues and maps is available at the entrance and at the bookshop.

Radical refurbishment has been completed in recent years, including the building of a vast new underground reception and service area, covered by the controversial pyramid in the Napoleon courtyard. The former Finance Ministry wing has been totally stripped out, and converted to still more galleries.

If you want a good introduction to the Louvre collections, consider taking a guided tour. Tours in English covering a selection of the highlights leave frequently from the ground floor information stand.

The museum is divided into the following main departments: Greek and Roman Antiquities; Oriental Antiquities; Egyptian Antiquities; Sculpture; Objets d'Art and Furniture; Painting; Drawing.

Since 1995 the Louvre has rated as the world's largest museum, overtaking the Metropolitan in New York, and the Hermitage in St Petersburg. Excavation work has opened up the superbly preserved foundations of the original fortress. The moat and inner keep or donjon formed part of a medieval castle which later was demolished.

A museum shop sells reproductions, etc.

Open: Summer – Thursday to Sunday 9-18 hrs. Monday and Wednesday until 21.45 hrs. Winter – Main collection: 09.45-18.30 hrs (other rooms close 17.00 hrs). Closed Tuesdays. Cost 45F until 15 hrs; then 26F and on Sundays. Free for under-18s. Free on first Sunday of each month.

Métro: Palais-Royal/Louvre

Musée d'Orsay, 7e – Quay Anatole France

The new Musée d'Orsay should certainly be on the not-to-be-missed list for someone visiting Paris for the first (or umpteenth) time, and as such it is often crowded.

In terms of both its art collection and its popularity it ranks next to the Louvre among the wealth of Paris Museums. Its greatest prize is the world's best collection of Impressionist and Post-Impressionist paintings.

The museum has been a huge success since it opened in 1986. It occupies a converted railway station and station hotel – the station being a marvellous building stunningly restored. It provides a vast area of exhibition space on three floors of galleries and halls.

The museum is devoted to art of the period 1848 to 1914. Most of the best of 19th and early 20th century art from other Paris museums (including the Louvre) was moved to the Musée d'Orsay. As well as painting and sculpture, it covers the range of 19th century art and design – including photography, architecture, and graphic design.

If you leave the Louvre you must buy another ticket to return on the same day. At the Musée d'Orsay you can return on the same ticket.

Open: 10.00-18.00 hrs. Closed Mondays. Open till 21.45 on Thursday; from 09.00 hrs on Sundays.

Cost 36F (reduced 24F – under 18 free).

Métro: Musée d'Orsay/Assemblée Nationale

Pompidou Centre – The Beaubourg, 4e

The Beaubourg Centre (as the Pompidou Centre is popularly known) was built as a national centre for modern art and culture in every field. It took off the moment it was opened in 1977, outdoing the Louvre and the Eiffel Tower in the number of visitors it attracted (about 8 million people enter it in a year).

The novel and audacious high-tech appearance of the building is famous. The large Piazza in front of the Centre is the scene of continual acts and 'happenings' by street entertainers and artists. The whole area around buzzes with life.

The Beaubourg building houses the most important collection of modern art in Paris, and in fact the largest collection in the world: the Musée Nationale d'Art Moderne. Every important modern painter of the twentieth century is here. The Centre also has special exhibitions of contemporary art.

Entry to the Beaubourg building is free but the museum and major exhibitions have admission charges.

The building has many other multi-media facilities. There is a bookshop with a very extensive selection of postcards and posters on the ground floor. On the top floor is a self-service restaurant with a five-star view – see Chapter 15.

Open: Weekdays (except Tuesday): 12.00-22.00 hrs Saturday and Sunday: 10.00-22.00 hrs. Cost for Museum of Modern Art 35F. (16-24 yrs and over-65 24F.) Day passes available.

Note that the Centre will close in September 1997 for a £50 million refit in readiness for the millenium.

Métro: Hotel de Ville/Rambuteau/Châtelet

La Villette, 19e – Centre for Science and Industry (La Cité des Sciences et de l'Industrie).
Parc de la Villette

You may think that there is nothing uniquely Parisian about a science museum. But there is something particularly French about the imagination and assurance in the planning of this science centre. It is simply the best museum of its kind.

Opened in 1986, the building is an exciting piece of futuristic architecture. The sheer scale is awesome. It is set in a 74-acre park, ambitiously landscaped, with facilities for children. The displays are designed for active exploration and participation by the visitor, with hands-on displays. The museum abounds with innovative ideas.

The permanent exhibition named Explora, for which audio guides in English are available, has four themes: earth and the universe; life and the environment; matter and the work of man; and language and communication. There is an exhibition about the frontiers of French technology.

The Géode is a 112-foot diameter polished steel sphere which reflects the park in its mirrored walls. It houses a cinema with a semi-circular screen covering 10,562 square feet (1000 sq metres). Separate entrance to Géode 57F; 44F reduced.

La Villette is situated on the outskirts of Paris, but there are hours of interest here for anyone with an interest in science and technology. Children enjoy the discovery and activity centre.

Open: 10.00-18.00 hrs. Closed Mondays. Cost: 50F; 35F under-25s and over-60s. Under-7's free.

Métro: Porte de la Villette/Porte de Pantin

Chapter Six

Other places to see

For convenience, the main buildings, monuments, museums and parks and gardens are listed below by category in alphabetical order. Most national museum rates are reduced for under-24s and for the over-60's. Many museums offer half price on Sundays. Prices and entrance times change frequently, so check first before making a special journey.

6.1 Buildings and Monuments

Alexandre III Bridge

Built for the 1900 World Exhibition this superb bridge, in the style of the Belle Epoque, was inaugurated by Tsar Alexandre III.   **Métro:** Invalides

Arc de Triomphe   See Chapter 5.

Conciergerie, 4e – Quai de L'Horloge

An imposing 14th century Gothic building where you can see the prison cells of Robespierre and Danton and other reminders of the French Revolution.
Open: 9.30-18.00 summer; 10-17 hrs winter. Entrance 28F, (reduced 18F).   **Métro:** Cité

Ecole Militaire, 7e

Regarded by many as one of the finest pieces of 18th century architecture, this forms the southern boundary of the Champs de Mars. Napoleon received part of his military training here and it is still used by the Army as an officers' training college. It is closed to the public.   **Métro:** Ecole Militaire

Eiffel Tower   See Chapter 5.

Fountain of the Innocents, 1er

On the south-east part of the Forum des Halles.
Sculpted by Jean Goujon in 1550.

Métro: Les Halles

The Madeleine, 8e – Place de la Madeleine

Named after St Mary Magdalen and built in the style
of a Greco-Roman temple, this church is particularly
lovely at night.   **Métro:** Madeleine

Montparnasse Tower   See Chapter 15.

Notre-Dame Cathedral   See Chapter 5.

Opera House, 9e - Place de l'Opéra

Designed by Garnier and built in 1875, the Second
Empire facade is one of the most famous sights of
Paris. The entrance hall and reception rooms can be
visited daily. Open 10-17 hrs. Entrance 30F (reduced
18F). Guided visits 60F.   **Métro:** Opéra

Palais de Chaillot, 16e – Place du Trocadéro

This palace was built in 1937 to house not a monarch
but museums and the National Theatre. The terrace
affords the best view of gardens and fountains of the
Trocadéro, the Seine, the Eiffel Tower, the Champs
de Mars and the Ecole Militaire beyond.

Métro: Trocadéro

Palais de Justice, 1er

On the Ile de la Cité, opening off the Boulevard du
Palais. In the 13th century this was a royal palace
but became a court and was renamed during the
Revolution. Prisoners from the Conciergerie were
brought here for trial. The public are admitted to
hearings of civil cases and trials for minor offences.
Open: 9-18 hrs, except weekends.   **Métro:** Cité

The Palais Royal, 1er

Designed in 1639 for Richelieu, it was bequeathed by
him to Louis XIII and inhabited by lesser members

of the Royal Family. During the Revolution the grounds became the haunt of prostitutes and gamblers. Now it is an area of book and antique shops.

Métro: Palais Royal

The Pantheon, 5e

Formerly a church, this building became in 1791 a resting place for the great freethinkers of France. Among those enshrined here are Mirabeau, Voltaire, Rousseau, Victor Hugo and Zola.
Open: 9.30-18-30 summer; 10.00-17.30 hrs winter.
Entrance: 32F; students 21F.   **Métro:** Luxembourg

The Pont Neuf, 1er

The oldest bridge in Paris. Started in 1578 and completed in 1604.   **Métro:** Pont Neuf

Sacré Coeur   See Chapter 5.

Sainte Chapelle   See Chapter 5.

Sewers (Les Egouts de Paris), 7e

Something different: a tour of the sewers which departs from Place de la Résistance (7e) at the corner of Quai d'Orsay every day except Thursday and Friday, 11–17 hrs summer; 11-16 hrs winter.
This guided tour below the Paris streets costs 25F; students and children 20F.   **Métro:** Alma Marceau

6.2 Museums and Galleries

There are several hundred museums and galleries in Paris. Those listed below are merely a selection of the most popular and famous.

Most museums in Paris offer lower prices for children, under 24's and over 60's. You will need a passport or other identification to claim the reduction.

Otherwise, the best bet for museum devotees is to buy a Museum Pass – please check the details at end of Chapter 3.

Army Museum, 7e – Hotel des Invalides

One of the world's richest army museums.
Open: 10-18 hrs (Oct to March 10-17 hrs.)
Entrance 35F (reduced price 25F).   **Métro:** Varenne

Cluny Museum, 5e – 6 Place Paul-Painlevé

Medieval Art. The greatest treasure is the beautiful tapestry series called 'The Lady and the Unicorn'. Open: 09.15-17.45 hrs. Closed: Tuesday and Public Holidays. Entrance: 28F; reduced and Sundays 18F.
Métro: St-Michel

Costume Museum (Musée de la Mode et du Costume), 16e – 10 Avenue Pierre-1e-de-Serbie

A vast collection of fashion from 1735 to present. Open: May-August 10.00-17.40 hrs. Closed: Mon and Public Holidays. Entrance: 35F; children 25F.
Métro: Iéna

Decorative Arts Museum (Musée des Arts Decoratifs), 1er – Marsan Pavilion, 107 Rue de Rivoli

Represents all forms of decorative art from the Middle Ages to today, showing the changes in style and taste. Includes design, furniture, arts and crafts. Open: Wed-Sat 12.30-18.00 hrs, Sun 12.00-18.00 hrs. Closed Mon and Tue. Entrance: 25F (reduced 16F). **Métro:** Palais Royal/Louvre

Fashion and Textile Museum, 1er – Louvre

Now occupying three floors in the Greater Louvre Extension, this collection comprises 20,000 costumes and 35,000 accessories from the 17th century to the present day, and featuring important pieces by the major 20th haute couture designers. Open daily except Mon, 11-18 hrs (from 10 hrs on Sat & Sun. Wed open until 22 hrs. **Métro:** Louvre

Grévin Museum, 9e – 10 Boulevard Montmartre

The main Paris waxworks, with many historical scenes. Open: 13-18 hrs; 10-18 hrs in school holidays. Entrance: 50F (reduced 36F).
Métro: Rue Montmartre/Richelieu-Drouot

Grévin Museum, Forum des Halles, 1er

A waxworks display portraying Paris of the Belle Epoque (1885 to 1900). Delightfully done. (A branch of the Grévin Museum above, this is on Level 1 of the Forum).

Open: 14-18 hrs; 11-18 hrs in school holidays.
Closed Sunday.
Entrance: 42F (reduced 32F); children 6-14, 32F.
Métro: Châtelet Les Halles

Guimet Museum, 16e – 6 Place Iéna

Oriental art collection of surpassing excellence and world importance. Closed for renovation until end of 1998. **Métro:** Iéna

The Louvre See Chapter 5.

Maritime Museum, 16e – Palais de Chaillot

French sea power and shipping through the ages.
Open: 10.00-18.00 hrs. Closed: Tue. Entrance: 38F (reduced 25F). **Métro:** Trocadéro

Marmottan Museum, 16e – 2 Rue Louis-Boilly

Collection of works mainly by Monet, but also by a number of other Impressionists.
Open: 10.00-17.30 hrs. Closed Mon. Entrance: 35F (reduced 15F). **Métro:** La Muette

Musée Carnavalet, 3e – Hôtel Carnavalet, 23 Rue de Sévigné

Illustrates the history of Paris over the 400 years from the Renaissance to the Belle Epoque. It also preserves the apartments of Mme de Sévigné, the famous hostess and wit who lived here from 1677-96 during Louis XIV's time. The building itself, in the Marais, is a beautiful and historic mansion.
Open: 10.00-17.40 hrs. Closed Mon. Entrance: 27F (reduced 14.50F). **Métro:** St-Paul

Museum of Mankind, 16e – Palais de Chaillot

Illustrates lifestyles from different parts of the world.
Open: 09.45-17.15 hrs. Closed: Tue. Entrance: 30F (reduced 20F). **Métro:** Trocadero

Orangerie, 1er – Tuileries Gardens

Beautifully displayed collection of Impressionist and Post-Impressionist paintings.
Open: 09.45-17.00 hrs. Closed: Tue. Entrance: 28F (reduced 18F). **Métro:** Concorde

OTHER SIGHTS

Musée d'Orsay   See Chapter 5.

Palais de la Decouverte, 8e – Grand Palais

Museum of scientific discoveries and a planetarium, with live demonstrations of varied aspects of popular science.
Open: 09.30-18.00 hrs. Sun from 10-19 hrs. Closed Mon. Entrance: 25F (Planetarium 15F extra).

Métro: Franklin D Roosevelt

Petit Palais, 8e - Avenue Winston Churchill

Museum of fine arts, renowned for its outstanding contemporary exhibitions.
Open: 10.00-17.40 hrs. Closed: Mon. Entrance: 27F (reduced 14.50F).

Métro: Champs Elysées-Clémenceau

Picasso Museum, 3e
Hôtel Salé, 5 Rue de Thorigny

Works of Picasso are displayed from his own collection of paintings, ceramics and notable sculptures; also African masks, and works by contemporaries.
Open 09.30-17.30 hrs, Wed till 22 hrs. Closed Tue. Entrance: 28F (reduced 18F). Free under 18 yrs.

Métro: St-Paul/Chemin Vert/St-Sébastien

Pompidou Centre   See Chapter 5.

Rodin Museum, Hôtel Biron, 7e
77 Rue de Varenne.

Many of Rodin's finest sculptures in a lovely mansion and garden.
Open: 9.30-17.45 hrs summer; until 16.45 winter. Closed: Monday. Entrance: 28F (reduced 18F).

Métro: Varenne

Victor Hugo Museum, 4e – 6 Place des Vosges

Mementoes of the author's life and works including sketches for the 'Notre Dame de Paris' manuscripts. The restored dining room includes Chinese furniture brought from the house of his mistress in Guernsey.
Open: 10.00-17.40 hrs. Closed: Mon and Public Holidays. Entrance: 17.50F (reduced 9F).

Métro: Bastille

6.3 Parks and Gardens

Bois de Boulogne

Over 2000 acres of woods, lawns, boating lakes, amusement parks, zoo, racecourses, restaurants.

Métro: Les Sablons

Bois de Vincennes

Slightly further out of town but worth a visit if the weather's good: lake, woods, park zoo, racetrack, Indo-Chinese garden. **Métro:** Château de Vincennes

Botanical Gardens (Jardin des Plantes), 5e

Include a winter garden, an alpine garden, a menagerie of various birds, beasts and reptiles and over 10,000 classified plants; also the Natural History Museum. **Métro:** Gare d'Austerlitz/Jussieu

Luxembourg Gardens, 6e

The most extensive green open space on the Left Bank. **Métro:** Luxembourg

Palais Royal, 1er

Elegant walled garden. **Métro:** Palais Royal

Parc Monceau, 8e

Landscaped garden with many statues and trees based on an English garden. **Métro:** Monceau

Tuileries Gardens, 1er

Typically French formal gardens. **Métro:** Tuileries

Père-Lachaise cemetery, 20e

A huge town cemetery with 19th and 20th century tombs, some old and crumbling, others wildly imaginative. This is the resting place of many famous names: Chopin, Molière, Racine, Oscar Wilde, Proust, Balzac, Edith Piaf, Yves Montand to name but a few. **Métro:** Gambetta

Montmartre cemetery, 18e

Other famous people rest here including Baudelaire, Stendhal, Berlioz. **Métro:** Blanche

Chapter Seven
Out of Paris

Most tour operators offer choice of day excursions out of Paris – an informative and hasslefree way of exploring the regional highlights. Here's a short list to consider.

Versailles – 13 miles south-west of Paris

Built by the Sun King, Louis XIV, between 1661 and 1682, the palace of Versailles and its gardens and park comprise the world's most sumptuous royal residence. The scale and grandeur are overwhelming. The palace covers 27 acres; the gardens, 235 acres; the park beyond, 14,000 acres.

You could spend an enchanting day in the superbly landscaped and ornamented gardens, without setting foot in the palace. But at least you should see the State Apartments, the Hall of Mirrors and some of the private rooms.

Open daily except Mon and Public Holidays. Palace hours 09.00-17.30 hrs; May-Sep 09.00-18.30 hrs. Gardens open dawn to dusk. Cost: 45F, reduced 35F.

Fontainebleau – 40 miles south-west of Paris

Another royal palace, even lovelier than Versailles, but less majestic. The original 12th-century hunting lodge was converted into a majestic château by François I in the 16th century. Later monarchs made lavish additions.

The result is a rich variety of styles which display the evolution of French architecture and interior decor. The François I Gallery was decorated by leading Italian Renaissance artists and should not be missed. Also see the exquisite boudoir of Marie-Antoinette.

Fontainebleau is often much less crowded than Versailles, and guided tours are available.

Around the palace is the forest of Fontainebleau – 42,000 acres of woodland in a remarkable setting of dramatic rock formations.

Palace open daily 9.30-12.30, 14.00-17.00 hrs; closed Tue. Entrance: 32F (reduced 10F).

Disneyland Paris – 20 miles east of Paris

This magic world features the famous theme park attractions that draw millions of visitors annually in California, Florida and Tokyo. Disneyland Paris is divided into five zones: Main Street, USA; Frontierland; Adventureland; Fantasyland; and Discoveryland. You can meet famed movie stars like Mickey Mouse and Goofy.

The accent is on family entertainment, with around 40 major shows, rides and ride-through adventures which have all been consumer-tested in USA and Japan. These include "Pirates of the Caribbean", "It's a Small World", and the simulator-based space journey "Star Tours".

Access from Paris is by regional rail RER. By road, the Resort is reached along the A4 expressway that runs from Paris to Strasbourg.

Chantilly – 26 miles north of Paris

Among the attractions of Chantilly is a beautiful château set in a landscaped park. Inside the château, the Musée Condé displays an art collection with great masterpieces.

Close by is the famous racecourse. At stables in the area some 3000 thoroughbreds are trained each year. Horse-lovers enjoy visiting the 18th century stables which house the Living Museum of the Horse (Musée Vivant du Cheval), showing different breeds in the flesh and giving equestrian demonstrations.

Park and museums open daily, 10.30-17.30 hrs (Saturdays, Sundays and Bank holidays 10.30-18.00 hrs). March 1 to October 31 daily except Tuesday, 10.00-18.00 hrs.
1 Nov to 28 Feb – 10.30-12.45 and 14.00-17.00
Entrance: 35F, Park 15F, Children 9F.

Giverny – 52 miles north-west of Paris

Something special for art and garden lovers: a visit to the tiny village of Giverny, located where the Epte River meets the Seine. Here is the house and idyllic garden where the impressionist artist Claude Monet lived from 1883 until his death in 1926.

Monet's growing prosperity enabled him to buy land where he diverted river water to make a Japanese garden complete with an arched bridge, weeping willows and bamboo. His water-lily pond became the subject of a great series of paintings which recorded innumerable variations of light and colour, reflecting the time of day, the ever-changing cloud patterns or the different seasons.

In Paris the *Waterlily* series – donated by Monet to the nation in 1922 – is displayed in two rooms of the Musée de l'Orangerie.

Monet's house and garden are preserved in their original condition, except for the artist's huge studio which is used for the sale of souvenirs. The house museum is open April-October, 10-12 and 14-18 hrs daily except Monday. The gardens are open year-round.

Chartres – 55 miles south-west of Paris

Well worth the journey, to see one of the greatest cathedrals of the Middle Ages. After your visit, explore the narrow hilly streets, and make time for the stained-glass centre at 5 rue de Cardinal Pie. (Centre International du Vitrail – open 10–18 hrs, closed lunch time. Entrance: 10F.)

Chapter Eight

Shopping

8.1 The pleasure of shop-gazing

Paris is one of the greatest shopping centres in the world – and it comes top as the most seductive. Shopkeepers from the most modest to the grandest can create that special allure. Glamour is in the air.

Shopping and window shopping are among the highlights of any visit to Paris. The Parisian sense of display is a perpetual delight, with some of the window dressing reaching ravishing heights. More down-to-earth, you can enjoy the exuberance and character of the street markets.

The most typical aspect of Paris shopping is the number of small shops of individuality. There are also grand department stores, but it is the range and character of the boutiques that gives the special style and colour to this great garden of shopping.

Prices

The articles in Paris shops are often more expensive than in Britain or America, but offer good value if you know where to look. Possibly it's worth paying the higher price for quality, fashion or design. Many shops will gift-wrap at no extra charge.

Sizes

For women's dresses and suits, these are sizes for the equivalent French, UK and US measurements.

France	36N	38N	40N	42N	44N	46N	48
Britain	10	12	14	16	18	20	22
USA	8	10	12	14	16	18	20

SHOPPING

Fashion and Clothes

For women's fashion, shopping in Paris still ranks first in the world.

Haute Couture

The highest pinnacles of women's fashion are the *grands couturiers,* the great designers and dress makers of *haute couture.* Two streets near the Champs-Elysées house many famous names: Avenue Montaigne (includes Christian Dior, Guy Laroche, Nina Ricci) and Rue du Faubourg Saint-Honoré.

Most of the other supreme names – Balmain, Ted Lapidus, Chanel, etc. – are within ten minutes' walk of these two streets, in particular Rue François ler, Avenue George V, and some side streets.

These haute couture houses also have boutiques, usually on the same premises, where you can buy handmade ready-to-wear clothes – at phenomenal prices. But walk around, look, and be enthralled.

Avant Garde Styles

For avant garde designers, the hottest centre is the Place des Victoires (2e), near Les Halles, with many exciting boutiques in the area. Another bright centre of new design is Saint-Germain-des-Prés on the Left Bank, especially the boutiques in the area of Rue de Grenelle and Rue du Cherche-Midi, 7e.   **Métro:** Sèvres-Babylone/Rue du Bac/St-Germain-des-Prés.

More Fashion Shopping

There are original and beguiling boutiques all around Paris. If you want to look at the new fashions, don't forget the great department stores, Galeries Lafayette and Printemps, described below and in Chapter 5.

Bargain and Discount Stores

Paris has more and better shops specialising in discount and secondhand clothing of quality than any other city in Europe. Many of these shops deal in designer clothes at far below their original price.

Last season's designer garments from fashion houses may sell at half price. If you see the word *dégriffés*, it means 'without label', and they will be heavily discounted.

The original café society.

Paris is famed for its glamorous nightlife.

Cruises along the Seine are a popular and inexpensive way to see many of the major sights.

The Pompidou Centre

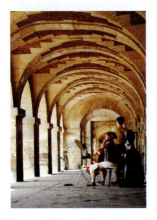

Pavement cafés line the Champs Élysées. Dining here can prove to be an expensive experience.

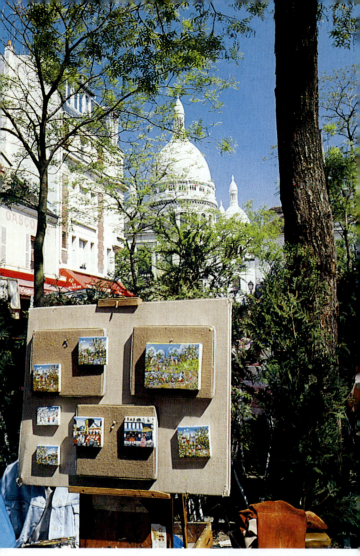

Street artists take inspiration from the Sacré Coeur.

*Even Parisian
postcards ooze
sophistication.*

A trip to Paris isn't complete without a visit to the Eiffel Tower.

IM Pei's glass pyramid is the entrance to arguably the world's most famous museum - the Louvre.

Like most major cities, Paris is as vibrant during the night as it is during the day.

The 3,300 year old Obelisk was donated to France by the Viceroy of Egypt in 1831.

Also look for the word *Soldes*: it means bargains or reductions. There are two streets on the Left Bank which are lined with shops specialising in *dégriffés* and *soldes*. The streets are:

- Rue Saint-Placide, 6e.   **Métro:** St Placide
- Rue Saint-Dominique, 7e.

       Métro: Latour Maubourg/Invalides

Paris is also well supplied with upmarket secondhand clothes shops. For the visitor, the easiest shop for buying secondhand clothes is probably Reciproque, at 95, 101 and 123 Rue de la Pompe, 16e. (Do investigate all three shops if you go.)

       Métro: Pompe/Victor Hugo

Another strong tip for high quality secondhand clothing – for women, children and men – is Cherche-minippes, 109-111 Rue du Cherche-Midi, 6e.

       Métro: Vaneau

8.2 Interesting shopping locations

Forum des Halles, 1er – Rue Pierre Lescot

The Forum is a pedestrian concourse of glass and aluminium which goes down four levels. Because of the design, all levels get natural light. It was opened in 1979 as a shopping and leisure complex. Over two hundred shops, a dozen cinemas, many cafés and restaurants are set around lively arcades. The Forum is very popular, with no need to take account of the weather above. It's a good place to hunt for presents. The area around is equally worth exploring.

       Métro: Les Halles/Châtelet - Les Halles

Rue Bonaparte and Rue des Saints-Pères, 6e

An excellent area for exotic antiques and high fashion boutiques. Good window shopping.

       Métro: St-Germain-des-Prés

Rue du Paradis 16e.

Lined with shops for porcelain, glass and tableware – makes quite an astonishing display. Don't miss the great Baccarat establishment which exhibits a dazzling collection of glass objects in the Musée du Cristal at No 30.

       Métro: Château d'Eau/Poissonnière

8.3 *Department stores*

Galeries Lafayette and Printemps
Boulevard Haussmann, 9e.

These two neighbouring department stores have information desks where English is understood. Both these stores keep at the leading edge of Paris shopping.

Although not cheap, prices are not excessive. Try to visit on weekday mornings when the stores are less crowded. Avoid Saturdays when they swarm with shoppers. Rest your feet with a coffee on the top floor and enjoy a fine view over Paris.

Both stores have a big reputation for fashion. The Galeries Lafayette devotes two floors to its fashion department, and more than 10,000 customers visit it every day. Fashion Shows are held every Wednesday at 11 a.m., and on Fridays Apr-Oct at 2.30 p.m.

Printemps likewise offers a 40-minute Fashion Show, free, every Tuesday at 10 a.m. Also on Fridays, Mar-Oct. **Métro:** Havre Caumartin/Auber

Aux Trois Quartiers – 23 Bd de la Madeleine, 1er

Attentive service and high quality goods in the most Parisian of shopping centres. Here is an arcade of 75 Boutiques that are linked to many of the greatest and most expensive names of fashion and beauty. The complex also includes a men's traditional fashion department called Madelios.
Open Mon-Sat 10-19 hrs. **Métro:** Madeleine

Au Bon Marché – 38 Rue de Sèvres, 7e

The oldest department store in Paris, and the only major one on the Left Bank. Has a superlative self-service food hall. Covers most shopping requirements at moderate prices. Also has an antiques department. Not very crowded. **Métro:** Sèvres-Babylone

La Samaritaine – 19 Rue de la Monnaie, 1er

An enormous family type department store in four huge buildings. Highly regarded particularly for practical clothes and working clothes and household items. Realistic or low prices. Open Wednesdays until 10 p.m.

Métro: Pont Neuf/Châtelet

8.4 Markets and supermarkets

Monoprix, Prisunic and Uniprix are chains of super-markets with several outlets throughout Paris. They offer a good selection of food and wine, clothes, cosmetics and household items, at reasonable or cheap prices and surprising quality. Larger branches stock many items suitable for presents. Branches of Nicolas carry a wide variety of wines and spirits.

Street markets abound in Paris and are part of Paris life. There are open air markets selling antiques, stamps, flowers, and much else. Above all, there are markets for food.

Street Food Markets

Everyone should go to a street food market for an insight into a fascinating aspect of Parisian lifestyle. Early morning is best to visit food markets. The sellers set up their stands by 8 a.m., and stop at 13 hrs. Then they re-open from 16 hrs until 19.30 hrs.

Nearly all markets are closed Mondays; and some on Sundays, while others are open Sunday mornings. Wherever you stay in Paris, there'll be a local market which may be as interesting as those which are more famous. Here are some well-known markets:

Rue Cler, 7e

Bustling with vitality – a fine example of a Parisian street market, though distinctly classy. runs from Avenue de la Motte-Picquet to the Rue de Grenelle. Near the Invalides and the Eiffel Tower. Open Tuesday to Saturday.   **Métro:** Ecole Militaire

Rue de Buci and Rue de Seine, 6e

The most photographed street market and the most colourful. Very entertaining. Open Tuesday to Sunday.   **Métro:** St-Germain-des-Prés/Odéon

Rue Mouffetard, 5e

Extends from the Rue de l'Epée de Bois to the Carrefour des Gobelins, near the Latin Quarter. Explore the side streets as well. Open Tuesday to Sunday.
                    Métro: Censier Daubenton/Monge

Flower Markets

Place Lépine, Ile de la Cité, 4e
This is the most famous flower market, situated near Notre Dame. Open 8-19 hrs Mon-Sat. On Sundays the Place Lépine becomes a bird and pet market.

Métro: Cité

Madeleine Flower Market, 8e
This is held at the back of the Madeleine and is open daily except Mondays. **Métro:** Madeleine

Place des Ternes, 17e
Also has an excellent food market. Open Tue-Sun.

Métro: Ternes

Flea Markets

The flea markets – *marchés aux puces* – have been a well known feature of Paris. The days when they offered plenty of bargains have long since gone. Three of the most noteworthy are:

Marché aux Puces de Saint-Ouen – Porte de Clignancourt, 17e
If you go only for entertainment value, this is a good choice of market. As the largest flea market in Europe, extending for 4 miles, you cannot see it all in one visit. There's lots of junk, antiques, tourists and atmosphere. Open Sat, Sun & Mon 7-19 hrs.

Métro: Porte de Clignancourt

Porte de Vanves, 14e - Av Georges Lafenestre and Av Marc Sangnier
The Avenue Marc Sangnier has a good and cheap market for bric-a-brac. Round the corner in Avenue Lafenestre is the quality part of the market.
Open Sat-Sun 7-19 hrs.

Métro: Porte de Vanves

Porte de Montreuil
A pleasant market to wander around. The best flea market for secondhand clothes, including fashionable clothing from long ago. Open Sat, Sun & Mon 7-19 hrs. **Métro:** Porte de Montreuil

Chapter Nine
Eating and drinking

9.1 The food and drink choice

Paris is the gastronomic capital of the world. In no other city can be found such a good choice for eating out with real enjoyment. Moreover you will get better value for money than say in Britain, as standards in modest restaurants are much higher and prices are moderate.

Eating and drinking places in Paris can be classified as follows:

Restaurants: These are for proper meals (that is, lunch and dinner). Prices range from very cheap to extremely expensive. Very small restaurants are also called *bistros*.

A *brasserie* is part restaurant, part café – essentially it is a grander café.

Cafés are generally open all day, starting with coffee and croissants for breakfast. They will serve a more or less limited range of food (sandwiches, snacks, etc) and some offer a main meal, usually one *plat du jour*. They serve a wide variety of hot and cold drinks and wines, spirits and beer. They generally have both a bar counter and tables.

Café-tabacs are a variety of café which also sells tobacco, stamps, postcards, Métro tickets, etc., and are generally cheap. They have a maroon diamond-shaped sign outside.

Fashionable cafés can be very expensive.

Bars: There is no real distinction between most 'bars' and 'cafés' – the names are interchangeable. However, some bars have a smart, cocktail-style character and may have live music during the evening. These we will call Smart Bars, and they will be considered separately in the next chapter on 'Nightlife and Entertainment'. They are sometimes described as 'American Bars'.

Wine Bars are also quite distinct from other café-bars. There are a few 'pubs' and beer cellars serving beers on draught. The small number of *salons de thé* (tea rooms) usually open mid-morning for cakes and snacks. Most also serve wine. They are rather up-market and usually quite pricey.

The *Selfs* are self-service restaurants or cafeterias.

For take-away food, use the traditional French outlets. *Traiteur* (delicatessen) and *charcutier* (prepared meats) shops will offer a variety of interesting snacks and ready-to-eat dishes (*plats cuisine*). *Boulangeries* and *pâtisseries* (bread and pastry shops) are open until 7 pm.

Restaurants

If you don't want a full meal, go to a café (or *crêperie*, cafeteria, etc.), not to a restaurant.

Prices are always displayed outside every restaurant. The word *menu* in France means a set meal of more than one course with limited or no choice of dishes. *A la carte* refers to individually priced dishes any of which you may choose. Examine the prices and the choice of *menus* and *à la carte* dishes before you walk in.

It is usually much cheaper and better value to choose the fixed price menu (*menu prix fixe*) than to eat *à la carte*. You may be charged extra if you change an item on this menu, even a vegetable. On the other hand, opting for *à la carte* will offer you much greater choice, but the *plat du jour* is often the best choice in more modest restaurants.

You can order a jug of drinking water from the tap free in any restaurant or café – ask for *une carafe d'eau*. Sometimes wine or mineral water is included in the menu prix fixe. Remember extras can mount up surprisingly. Address the waiter politely as 'monsieur' or 'mademoiselle', and ask for advice whenever you want it.

Service is usually slower and meals more leisurely in France than is generally the case in Britain and

America. Reckon to wait for a dish to be freshly prepared.

A compulsory service charge of 15% is included in the advertised prices of all restaurants and cafés in Paris. It is at your discretion whether to leave an extra tip. Normally up to 10% is expected.

Many restaurants close on Sundays or Mondays. At the better known establishments, it is advisable to book in advance, particularly at weekends.

Selection of Restaurants

You will find excellent restaurants around practically every corner and down most side streets.

Regarding prices: you can spend more or less money in a restaurant according to your choice. Because of this, we have adopted a grading system which allows for an average complete meal.

£ – under £10 and frequently less.
££ – £10-£20.
£££ – £20+

Following is a short selection of restaurants which we can recommend from each arrondissement.

1er Arrondissement

Yakitori – 34 Place du Marché St Honoré   £
Tel: 01 42 61 03 54   **Métro:** Tuileries
Open until 22.45. Traditional Japanese brochettes.

Le Bistro d'Hubert – 36 Place du Marché St Honoré   £££
Tel: 01 42 60 03 00   **Métro:** Tuileries
Open until 22 hrs. Closed Sun. Excellent traditional cuisine.

Le Petit Goulot – 20 Rue du Roule   £
Tel: 01 42 36 72 52   **Métro:** Châtelet/Louvre
Open 12.00-14.30/19.00-22.30 hrs (not Sun & Mon) Generous helpings, traditional cooking.

Les Bouchons – 19 Rue des Halles   ££
Tel: 01 42 33 28 73   **Métro:** Châtelet
Open 12-01 hrs. 1920s decor. Brunch till 14 hrs.

2e Arrondissement

Le Drouot – 103 Rue de Richelieu £
Tel: 01 42 96 68 23   **Métro:** Richelieu-Drouot
Open until 21.30. Good value, very French, popular.

Le Vaudeville – 23 Rue Vivienne £££
Tel: 01 40 20 04 62   **Métro:** Bourse
Open 12-15.30 hrs., 19-04 hrs. 1920s style traditional cuisine, oysters and fresh foie gras.

4e Arrondissement

Le Canaille – 4 Rue Crillon £
Tel: 01 42 78 09 71   **Métro:** Sully Moreland
Open 11.45-14.15 & 19.30-23.00 hrs (closed Sat/Sun midday). Old Bistro style, set 3-course menu.

La Table des Gourmets – 14 Rue de Lombard ££
Tel: 01 40 27 00 87   **Métro:** Hôtel de Ville
Open 12-14.30 & 17-23 hrs. Closed Sunday lunch. Charming setting. Recommended by Thomson. Special priced menu available.

Le Quincambosse - 13 Rue Quincamploix ££
Tel: 01 42 78 68 48   **Métro:** Châtelet/Les Halles
Open daily 12-17 hrs and 19-23 hrs. Simple cooking, good quiches and salads attractively presented.

Bofinger – 5 Rue de la Bastille ££
Tel: 01 42 72 87 82   **Métro:** Bastille
Open 12-15 hrs & 18.30–01.00 hrs. Authentic art nouveau style brasserie. Traditional French seafood.

Taverne du Sergeant Recruteur ££
41 Rue St Louis en l'Ile.
Tel: 01 43 54 75 42   **Métro:** St Paul/Pont Marie
Open 19.00 – midnight. Do not serve lunch. Closed Sunday. Limitless wine and starters.

Les Caves du Marais St Catherine – 5 Rue Caron
Tel: 01 42 72 39 94   **Métro:** St Paul
Intimate cellar restaurant, candlelight and classical music. Excellent hors d'oeuvres buffet. ££

5e Arrondissement

La Ferme St Geneviève - 40 Rue de la Montagne St
Geneviève   £
Tel: 01 43 54 49 85   **Métro:** Maubert Mutualité
Open daily, closed Monday lunchtime.
Regional specialities, simple cooking.

Le Grenier de Notre Dame - 18 Rue de la Bûche-
rie. Tel: 01 43 29 98 29   **Métro:** St Michel
Open daily 12.00-14.30 & 19.30-22.45 hrs.
One of the best vegetarian restaurants.   £

L'Atelier Maître Albert – 1 Rue Maître Albert   ££
Tel: 01 46 33 06 44   **Métro:** Maubert Mutualité
Open 19.30-24.00 hrs, closed Sunday.   A beautiful
fireside setting. Excellent cooking.

La Cochonaille – 21 Rue de la Harpe   ££
Tel: 01 46 33 96 81   **Métro:** St Michel
Open daily 12-14 hrs and 18.30-24.00 hrs.
Traditional restaurant with a wide choice of menus.

6e Arrondissement

La Cour St Germain – 156 Bd St Germain   £
Tel: 01 43 26 85 49   **Métro:** St-Germain-des-Prés
Open daily until 00.30. Interesting starters, mouth-
watering desserts and steaks. Excellent value.

Restaurant des Beaux Arts – 11 rue Bonaparte   £
Tel: 01 43 26 92 64   **Métro:** St-Germain-des-Prés
Open daily 12.00-14.30 hrs., 19.00-22.45 hrs.
Excellent value. Haunt of many students and artists.

L'Assiette au Beurre – 11 Rue St Benoît   ££
Tel: 01 42 60 87 41   **Métro:** St-Germain-des-Prés
Open daily 12-15 & 19-23 hrs.
Good value, popular and noisy.

Closerie de Lilas – 171 Bd Montparnasse   ££
Tel: 01 43 26 70 50   **Métro:** Port Royal
Open daily 12.00-02.00 hrs. Renowned for its sea-
foods. Hemingway used to eat here!

Les Jardins St Benoît – 20 bis Rue St Benoît   ££
Tel: 01 42 22 48 10   **Métro:** St-Germain-des-Prés
Open daily 12.00-14.15 & 19-24 hrs.
Very good food, well presented in a pleasant setting.

Brasserie Lipp – 151 Bd St Germain   ££
Tel: 01 45 48 53 91   **Métro:** St Michel
Open 12-01 hrs. Closed first 3 weeks of August.
Classical Brasserie. Traditional venue of politicians
and academics.

7e Arrondissement

La Petite Chaise – 36 Rue de Grenelle   ££
Tel: 01 42 22 13 35   **Métro:** Sèvres Babylone
Open 12-14 & 19-23 hrs. A fashionable, 17th-century
style restaurant.

Leo Le Lion – 23 Rue Duvivier   ££
Tel: 01 45 51 41 77   **Métro:** Ecole Militaire
Open 12.30-14.00 hrs & 19.15-23.00 hrs. Closed Sat
and Sun in Nov/Dec. Excellent cooking from the
Lyon region of France.

Le Petit Niçois – 10 Rue Amélie   ££
Tel: 01 45 51 83 65   **Métro:** La Tour Maubourg
Open 12-14 hrs & 19.00-22.30 hrs. Closed Sunday
and Monday midday. Friendly atmosphere, good fish.

8e Arrondissement

L'Assiette au Boeuf – 123 Av des Champs Elysées
Tel: 01 47 20 01 13   £
    Métro: Charles de Gaulle-Etoile
Open until 01.00. Basic menu at reasonable prices.

La Rotonde – 12 Place St Augustin   ££
Tel: 01 45 22 33 05   **Métro:** St Augustin
Open daily until midnight.
Art Deco interior. Meat and seafood specialities.

Le Salardais – 2 Rue de Vienne   ££
Tel: 01 45 22 23 62   **Métro:** St Augustin
Open 12-23.30 hrs. Closed Sun. Traditional cuisine.

Boeuf sur le Toit – 34 Rue du Colisée £££
Tel: 01 43 59 83 80   **Métro:** Franklin D Roosevelt
Open until 02.00 hrs.
Spectacular Art Deco interior. Excellent seafood.

Café du Roy – 13 Rue Royale £££
Tel: 01 42 65 48 70   **Métro:** Concorde/Madeleine
Open daily until midnight.
Elegant restaurant with delicious food and wines.

9e Arrondissement

Chartier – 7 Rue du Faubourg-Montmartre £
Tel: 01 47 70 86 29   **Métro:** Rue Montmartre
Open 11-15 hrs & 18.30-21.30 hrs. A 19th-century
'bouillon' (popular restaurant) delightfully preserved.
Food is basic and cheap. An entertaining restaurant.

Chez Maurice – 44 Rue Notre Dame de Lorette ££
Tel: 01 48 74 44 86   **Métro:** St Georges
Open daily 12-15 hrs & 18.30 to midnight.
Good French cooking.

Charlot – 81 Boulevard de Clichy £££
Tel: 01 48 74 49 64   **Métro:** Clichy
Open daily 12-15 hrs & 19-01 hrs. Pricey but one of
the best shellfish restaurants in Paris. Must reserve.

10e Arrondissement

L'Enchotte Wine Bar – 11 Rue De Charrol £
Tel: 01 48 00 05 25   **Métro:** Poissonière
Open daily 10-23 hrs except Sun and Sat evening.
Snacks and meals served, wide selection of wines.

La Taverne de la Bière – 15 Rue de Dunkerque £
Tel: 01 42 85 12 93   **Métro:** Gare du Nord
Open until 02 hrs. Huge selection of beers. Good
sauerkraut and French and Alsatian food.

Terminus Nord – 23 Rue de Dunkerque £££
Tel: 01 42 85 05 15   **Métro:** Gare du Nord
Open until midnight. 1925 Brasserie, specializing in
oysters, seafood and sauerkraut.

Julien – 16 Rue du Faubourg St Denis £££
Tel: 01 47 70 12 06   **Métro:** Strasbourg St Denis
Open 12-15 hrs & 19.00-01.30 hrs. Brasserie with
Art Nouveau interior. Excellent food, speciality fish.

Chez Flo – 7 Cour des Petites Ecuries £££
Tel: 01 47 70 13 59   **Métro:** Strasbourg St Denis
Open daily until 02.00 hrs. Famous restaurant. Ex-
cellent fish. Oysters are their speciality.

11e Arrondissement

Jacques Melat – 42 Rue Léon-Frot £
Tel: 01 43 70 59 27   **Métro:** Charonne
Open 08.00-19.30 hrs., Tues and Thurs 11-22 hrs.,
closed Sun and Mon. Rustic cooking, simple, tasty.

Le Thermomètre – 4 Place de la République £
Tel: 01 47 00 30 78   **Métro:** République
Open daily 12-17 hrs & 19-01 hrs. Brasserie.

12e Arrondissement

La Connivence – 1 Rue de Cotte £
Tel: 01 46 28 46 17   **Métro:** Ledru Rollin
Open 12-14 & 20-23 hrs. Friendly bistro, traditional.

Le Morvan – 22 Rue Chaligny ££
Tel: 01 43 07 47 66   **Métro:** Reuilly Diderot
Open 12.00-14.30 & 19.30-21.30 hrs. A charming
bistro with owner-chef, Morvan regional cooking.

13e Arrondissement

Chez Françoise – 12 Rue de la Butte aux Cailles £
Tel: 01 45 80 12 02   **Métro:** Corvisart
Open 12-14 hrs & 19.30-22.00 hrs. Closed Sundays.
Excellent duck pâté and cassoulet.

Les Algues – 66 Ave des Gobelins ££
Tel: 01 43 31 58 22   **Métro:** Place d'Italie
Open 12-14 hrs & 19.30–22.30 hrs. closed Sun/Mon.
Specialises in seafood. The menu is changed daily.

14e Arrondissement

Art et Buffet – 16 Rue de la Grande Chaumière £
Tel: 01 46 34 24 16   **Métro:** Vavin
Open daily 12-14 hrs., 19.00-23.30 hrs.
Delicious quiches and salads. Bright and airy.

Chez Brebert – 71 Bld du Montparnasse   £
Tel: 01 42 22 55 31   **Métro:** Montparnasse
Open daily 12-15 & 19-02 hrs. Excellent couscous.

La Coupole – 102 Bld du Montparnasse   ££
Tel: 01 43 20 14 20   **Métro:** Vavin
Open until 02.00 hrs. A famous landmark. Notice the
decor, some by Toulouse Lautrec. Dancing in the
evenings. Good fish dishes.

15e Arrondissement

Le Commerce – 51 Rue du Commerce   £
Tel: 01 45 75 03 27   **Métro:** Commerce
Open 12-24 hrs. Quick, authentic French cooking.
Related to Chartier Restauraunt (9e Arrondissement)
but fewer tourists here.

Ashoka – 5 Rue Dr Jacquemarie-Clemence   £
Tel: 01 45 32 96 46   **Métro:** Commerce
Closed Monday lunchtime and Sunday.
An excellent Indian restaurant, Tandoori a speciality.

Hippopotamus – 12 Avenue du Maine   £
Tel: 01 42 22 36 75   **Métro:** Montparnasse
Open until 01.00 hrs.

Le Ciel de Paris – Montparnasse Tower, 56th Floor
Tel: 01 45 38 52 35   **Métro:** Montparnasse
Open 12-14.30 & 19-23.30 hrs. Magnificent views
over Paris; romantic setting. Wise to book ahead. ££

L'Orient Express – 4 Ave de la Porte de Sèvres
Tel: 01 45 57 26 27   **Métro:** Balard
Open 12-14.30 & 19.30-22 hrs. Closed Sun/Mon.
This superb restaurant is an authentic carriage of the
famous train. First class service, excellent seafood.

16e Arrondissement

Brasserie Stella – 143 Avenue Victor Hugo   ££
Tel: 01 45 53 02 68   **Métro:** Victor Hugo
Open 11.30-15.00 hrs & 19-24 hrs. Closed Sunday.

Le Cotton – 73 Avenue Kléber   ££
Tel: 01 47 27 73 75   **Métro:** Trocadero/Boissière
Open 11-02 hrs. Closed Sunday.
Good French food. Recommended by Thomson.
Special priced menus bookable from your Thomson
reps.

17e Arrondissement

Chez Natasha – 35 Rue Guersant
Tel: 01 45 74 23 86   **Métro:** Ternes
Open 12-15 & 19.30-23.30 hrs., closed Saturday and
Sunday lunch.
Buffet hors d'oeuvres, wine from the barrel.

Hippopotamus – 46 Avenue Wagram   £
Tel: 01 46 22 16 14   **Métro:** Ternes/Etoile
Open until 01.00 hrs.
Excellent value steaks.

L'Amanguier – 43 Ave des Ternes   ££
Tel: 01 43 80 19 28   **Métro:** Ternes
Open 12.00-14.30 & 19-24 hrs.
Lively, popular and good food.

Le Relais de Venise – Corner of Bvd Pereire   ££
Tel: 01 45 74 27 97   **Métro:** Porte Maillot
Open 12.00-14.30 & 19.00-23.45 hrs.
The best steaks you'll ever taste! It's steak or nothing
here but you won't wish for anything else. No reser-
vations, so go early – it's very popular.

La Marée – 1 Rue Daru   £££
Tel: 01 47 63 52 42   **Métro:** Ternes
Open 12.00-14.15 & 20.00-22.15 hrs. Closed Satur-
day & Sunday.
Reservations recommended. Excellent crayfish, deli-
cious sauces.

18e Arrondissement

Au Grain de Folie – 24 Rue de la Vieuville   £
Tel: 01 42 58 15 57   **Métro:** Abbesses
Open daily 12.00-23.30 hrs.
Imaginative vegetarian dishes, warm local atmosphere.

La Refuge des Fondues – 17 Rue Trois Frères   £
Tel: 01 42 55 22 65   **Métro:** Abbesses
Open daily, two sittings 18.30, 20.30 hrs.
Choice of meat or cheese fondue. Young, lively atmosphere. The wine is served in baby bottles.

Au Clair de la Lune – 9 Rue Poulbot   ££
Tel: 01 42 58 97 03   **Métro:** Abbesses
Closed Sunday and Monday lunch.
A romantic Montmartre restaurant. Nouvelle cuisine.

Wepler – 14 Place de Clichy   ££
Tel: 01 45 22 53 24   **Métro:** Place de Clichy
Open daily 12.00-01.00 hrs.
Renowned brasserie. Fresh shellfish a speciality.

Le Montmartre – 74 Rue Des Martyrs   ££
Tel: 01 42 51 17 45   **Métro:** Pigalle
Open daily 12-14 hrs & 18.30-22.30 hrs.
A bubbling brasserie serving good traditional French food.

9.2 Guide to Menu Items

Les Viandes	**Meat**
Agneau	Lamb
Aiguillette de boeuf	Braised beef
Andouillette	Tripe
Blanquette de veau	Casseroled veal with thick, creamy sauce
Boeuf	Beef
Boeuf Bourguignon	Beef cooked in red wine
Brochettes	Spit-cooked or barbecued meat (on skewers)
Carbonnade de boeuf	Casseroled beef
Cervelle	Brains

Châteaubriant	Fillet steak
Coeur	Heart
Contrefilet	Sirloin
Côtes de boeuf	Ribs of beef
Côtes/côtelettes	Chops
Entrecôte minute	Thin steak
Entrecôte au poivre	Pepper steak
Epaule de mouton	Shoulder of lamb
Escalope de veau	Veal escalope
Escargots	Snails
Filet	Fillet
Foie	Liver
Gigot d'Agneau	Leg of lamb
Jambon	Ham
Langue	Tongue
Museau de Porc	Pig's snout
Pavé	Steak
Paupiettes de veau	Rolled stuffed veal pieces
Porc	Pork
Pot au feu	Meat & vegetable stew
Ris de veau	Sweetbreads
Rognon	Kidney
Rôti	Roast
Selle d'Agneau	Saddle of lamb
Tranche	Top of the rump (also means 'slice')
Veau	Veal

Gibier et Volaille — Game & Poultry

Becasse	Woodcock
Caille	Quail
Canard	Duck
Chevreuil	Venison
Civet de lapin/lievre	Jugged rabbit/hare
Coq au vin	Chicken in red wine
Faisan	Pheasant
Lapin	Rabbit
Lievre	Hare
Oie	Goose
Perdrix	Partridge
Pintade	Guinea hen
Poulet basquaise	Basque chicken
Poussin farci	Stuffed chicken
Sanglier	Wild Boar

Les Poissons	Fish
Anguille	Eel
Brochet	Pike
Cabillaud/Morue	Cod/Salt Cod
Eperlan	Whitebait
Hareng	Herring
Macquereau	Mackerel
Merlan	Whiting
Meunière	Floured and buttered
Mulet	Mullet
Poché	Poached
Quenelles	Pike mousse/fish balls
Raie	Skate
Rouget	Red mullet
Saumon	Salmon
Sole	Sole
Thon	Tuna
Truite	Trout
Turbot	Turbot
à la vapeur	Steamed

Les Fruits de Mer	Shellfish
Belons	Type of large oyster
Bouillabaisse	Fish stew
Calamares	Squid
Coquilles St Jacques	Scallops
Crabe/Tourteau	Crab
Crevette	Shrimp
Ecrevisse	Crayfish
Fines Claires	Type of small oyster
Homard	Lobster
Huitres	Oysters
Langouste	Lobster
Langoustine	Large prawn
Moules (marinières)	Mussels (stewed in a delicious sauce)
Poulpe	Octopus
Praire	Clam
La soupe de poisson	Fish soup

Les Légumes	Vegetables
Ail	Garlic
Artichaut	Artichoke
Asperge	Asparagus

Betterave	Beetroot
Cèpes/Champignons	Mushrooms
Choucroute	Sauerkraut
Chou-fleur	Cauliflower
Cornichon	Gherkin
Cresson	Watercress
Crudités	Salad of raw vegetables
Chips	Crisps
Endive	Chicory
Epinards	Spinach
Fenouil	Fennel
Haricots Verts	French beans
Navet	Turnip
Oignon	Onion
Petits pois	Peas
Poireau	Leek
Poivre	Pepper for seasoning
Poivron	Red/green pepper
Pommes allumettes	Thin chips
Pommes frites	Chips
Pommes de terre	Potatoes
Salade Niçoise	Salad: tuna, olive, egg, tomato, etc
Salade verte	Green salad
Truffes	Truffles

Les Desserts — **Desserts**

Ananas	Pineapple
Charlotte	Fruit interior – sponge exterior
Clafoutis	Flan
Coulis	Sauce made from strained fresh fruit
Coupe de la Maison	Usually ice cream, fruit & cream
Crêpe	Pancake
Fraise/Fraises des bois	Strawberry/wild strawberries
Framboise	Raspberry
Fruits en saison	Fruits in season
Gaufre	Waffle
Glace	Ice cream
Ile flottante	Whipped egg whites floating in a custard sauce
Marrons glacés	Puréed chestnuts

Mousse au chocolat	Chocolate mousse
Parfait	Chocolate ice cream
Pêche	Peach
Poire Belle Hélène	Pear topped with hot chocolate sauce
Pomme	Apple
Sorbet	Water ice (Parisian speciality)
Tarte aux fruits	Open fruit pie
Tarte aux pommes	Open apple pie

Les Boissons   **Drinks**

Café	Small black coffee
Crème/café crème	White coffee
Express	Small, very strong black coffee
Thé	Tea (without milk)
Thé au citron/au lait	Tea with lemon/milk
Le lait	Milk
Un demi	Half of beer
Bière (à pression)	Beer (draught)
Vin rouge/blanc/rosé	Red/white/rosé wine
Pastis/Ricard/Anis /Anisette/Pernod	Aniseed-flavoured aperitif
Kir/Kir royal	Blackcurrant liqueur and white wine/champagne

Terms

Steak (etc): bleu	Very rare/blue
saignant	Rare
à point	Medium rare
moyen	Medium
bien cuit	Well done
L'addition s'il vous plaît	The bill please
La carte	The menu
Menu prix fixe	Fixed price menu
A la carte	Menu where you choose the dishes
Les hors d'oeuvres	Starters
Les entrées	First course
Le plat du jour	Main dish of the day

9.3 *The café lifestyle*

The café is an important feature of Paris, playing a vital part in the life of the city. Nowhere else on earth are cafés so highly developed or so various or so good.

They can be used by visitors for food, a wide variety of drinks, hot, soft, and alcoholic, the toilet (for the price of a cup of coffee), for the telephone; or for simply getting a flavour of French social life and talk. You can rest your feet there, revive the children (who are welcome in ordinary cafés) or idly enjoy watching the world go by as you sip your coffee or apéritif.

In the evenings people mostly go to cafés to drink and talk, rather than to eat.

There are two or frequently three tiers of prices in cafés. The cheapest is standing at the bar counter; next cheapest sitting near the bar; most expensive sitting on the terrace (or pavement in the summer).

You must not order your drinks at the bar, pay for them, and then sit down (as you would in an English pub) because of the difference in prices.

Every café displays a full price list. Examine it – especially before ordering less basic drinks like non-French beers or whisky.

Cafés in side streets are generally cheaper and less busy. Cafés close to popular tourist sights are more expensive and more occupied by tourists.

Café Selection

There are more than 10,000 cafés in Paris. It is beyond the scope of this guide to begin to list the more interesting ones. However, here are the names of a few famous ones – all of them expensive!

Les Deux Magots – 170 Boulevard St-Germain (6e)
Métro: St-Germain-des-Prés
Le Café Flore – Boulevard St Germain (6e)
Métro: St-Germain-des-Prés
La Périgourdine – Quai des Grand Augustins (5e)
Terrific band every night after 10 pm.
Métro: St Michel

Café de la Paix
Place de l'Opéra/Bd. des Capucines, 9e
Coffee approx. 23F, wonderful ice-cream (but expensive). **Métro:** Opera

Salons de Thé Selection

Angelina – 226 Rue de Rivoli, 1er
Open 10-19 hrs including Sundays; closed mid-July to mid-August. Provides aristocratic afternoon tea, delectable pastries, supreme hot chocolate, plus Belle Epoque decor. **Métro:** Tuileries/Concorde

Rose Thé – 91 Rue St Honoré, 1er
In a peaceful courtyard, surrounded by antique shops. Teas not too expensive.
Métro: Louvre/Châtelet-Les-Halles

La Pagode – 57 Bis Rue de Babylone, 7e
16-22 hrs. Tea in a beautiful pagoda; in summer in the Chinese garden. **Métro:** St Francis-Xavier

Tea Caddy – 14 Rue St Julien-le-Pauvre
Tea or coffee served in a very old house. In Latin Quarter, just across the bridge from Notre Dame. Moderate prices. Home-made cakes, scones and cinnamon toast. **Métro:** St Michel

Salon de Thé St-Louis – 81 Rue St Louis-en-l'Ile, 4e. 54 varieties of tea. **Métro:** Pont-Marie

Christian Constant – 26 Rue du Bac, 7e
Open 8-20 hrs. Tea room (19 kinds served) cum pastry and chocolate shop of exceptional quality.
Métro: Rue du Bac

Drinks

A common apéritif in Paris is kir. Kir is cassis (blackcurrant liqueur) with chilled white wine. Kir royale is cassis with sparkling wine.

Gin and tonic is not a recognised apéritif in Paris and is expensive. Vermouth, dry or sweet, is often favoured, e.g. Noilly Prat (dry and white) or Dubonnet (sweet and red).

Drinks without alcohol are very popular, such as the refreshing citron pressé (fresh lemon juice).

Chapter Ten

Paris After Dark

Paris has an international reputation for its nightlife. Apart from all the glamour, there is a sense of animation in Paris at night which is contagious.

Paris is supreme in the range and quantity of its nightly diversions – clubs, bars, discos, cabarets, revues and jazz cellars – all of which give it a unique social life, along with other forms of culture and entertainment. Here is the barest summary of the choice of activities to enjoy in Paris.

Strolling Around

The cheapest way to enjoy Paris after dark is to wander around and enjoy the street scenes, taking the occasional drink in sidewalk cafés. Among the more conspicuous spectacles are:

- entertainers around the Beaubourg Centre;
- the parade of latest fashions and exotic garb by streams of people in the area of Place St-Michel and neighbouring streets in the Latin Quarter;
- chic and showy pageant in the Champs-Elysées; chic and more class spectacle around the Opéra area; chic but also mixed and bohemian round the cafés and clubs in St-Germain-des-Prés and Montparnasse.

The seven main areas of nightlife are to be found in Champs-Elysées, Les Halles, Opéra, Montmartre (all Right Bank); and St-Germain-des-Prés, Montparnasse, and the Latin Quarter (all Left Bank).

Clubs

Clubs are generally very lively and crowded, with dancing a feature. Some have cabaret and revue.

There is also a generous choice of jazz and live rock clubs, while Paris is the centre of new African music. Latin-American music is also popular.

From youthful cellar clubs in the Latin Quarter where everyone might be freely welcome, to the renowned Regine's in the 8th arrondissement, the term 'club' can cover many different styles of nightlife.

Most evident of all are the 'discos', some of which are listed below.

Discothèques

The name 'discothèque' is applied widely and very loosely to many night spots. Discos range from the very stylish to the garish to the gimcrack. The more recognised ones are glitzy, supercharged, frenetic, and often galvanising. Here is a selection:

Olivia Valère – 40 Rue du Colisée, 8e
Tel: 01 42 25 11 68. 140F per drink; an exclusive club.   **Métro:** F D Roosevelt

Le Palace – 8 Rue du Faubourg Montmartre, 9e
Tel: 01 42 46 10 87. Open from 23 hrs.
Entrance 100F.   **Métro:** Rue Montmartre

La Scala – 188 bis Rue de Rivoli, 1er
Tel: 01 42 60 45 64. All welcome; free for girls Mon–Thu; Weekends, 80F.   **Métro:** Palais Royal

Le Bus Palladium – 6 Rue Fontaine, 9e
Tel: 01 48 74 54 99. Trendy place, closed Mon. Free Entry Tue-Thu; 120F Fri–Sun.
            Métro: Blanche

Fifth Avenue - 2 bis Avenue Foch, 6e
Tel: 01 45 00 00 13.
100F per drink. Exclusive club.   **Métro:** Etoile

La Locomotive – 90 Bd de Clichy, 18e
Tel: 01 42 57 37 37. Lively atmosphere; closed Mon; 60F weekday, 100F weekend. **Métro:** Blanche

Les Bains Douches – 7 Rue Bourg l'Abbé, 3e
Tel: 01 48 87 01 80. Fashion is the main attraction. Fun music. 140F entrance. **Métro:** Etienne Marcel

New York, New York – 27 Rue du Cadet Mouchette (4e) Tel: 01 43 21 48 96
Lively music and videos, closed Mondays, 60F weekdays, 100F weekends.   **Métro:** Montparnasse

Wine Bars

Relatively new in Paris, they are usually quite crowded and lively, serving a large choice of wine.

Le Rubis – 10 Rue Marché St-Honoré, 1er
Typically old-style Parisian, small and bustling; reasonable prices. **Métro:** Tuileries
L'Ecluse – 15 Place de la Madeleine, 8e
Well-known, and more expensive.**Métro:** Madeleine
A la Cloche des Halles – 28 Rue Coquillière, 1er
Marvellous choice of wines, informal; good prices.
Métro: Les Halles

Smart Bars

Cocktail/American-style bars are becoming very popular in Paris. The atmosphere is very different from the informal style cafés. People usually dress up and go for drinks before (or after) a show or club. These bars normally have a piano player. Here it's possible to escape the frantic pace of Paris by relaxing in lush, comfortable surroundings.

Some recommendations:

The American Bar – 56th Floor, Montparnasse Tower, Bd. Montparnasse
Approximate price for cocktails: 50-60F. Amazing views across Paris. **Métro:** Montparnasse-Bienvenue
L'Hôtel - 13 Rue des Beaux Arts, 6e
Very 'gentil' and quiet. This is where Oscar Wilde lived. **Métro:** St-Germain-des-Prés
Harry's Bar – 5 Rue Daunou, 2e
Piano bar with exotic cocktails. **Métro:** Opera
Paradis aux Fruits – Quai des Grand Augustins, 5e
Very good video bar with non-alcoholic cocktails.
Métro: St Michel
Les Trottoirs de Buenos Aires – 37 Rue des Lombards, 1er. Latin American dance show. Very good fun – try the tequila! **Métro:** Châtelet

Cabaret Shows

Paris has been famous for its cabaret shows for a hundred years (the Moulin Rouge opened in 1889). The best are excellent and expensive, maintaining a superb tradition of professional entertainment and well staged glamour.

Going to a top Parisian cabaret is a night out to remember. There are three categories of show:

• Where you see the performance just as in a theatre (e.g. Folies Bergère).

• Where you dine during the first performance and drink during the others (e.g. Lido, Moulin Rouge).

• Where you just watch and drink (Crazy Horse).

Generally, prices for the show start at 365F per person and will include a bottle of champagne between two (or two large drinks each). It's also possible to dine before the show at some cabarets. Prices start at 530F per person for basic menu, half bottle of wine, show and half bottle of champagne.

It is always necessary to make a reservation.

Some top-class cabarets are the following:

Paradis Latin – 28 Rue du Cardinal-Lemoine, 5e
Tel: 01 43 25 28 28.   **Métro:** Cardinal Lemoine
The most Parisian show of them all. Highly recommended. Spontaneous and slick, featuring a superb can-can sequence. Probably the best show in town. Dinner at 20.30; show at 21.45 hrs; closed Tuesday.

Lido – 116 bis Avenue des Champs Elysées, 8e
Tel: 01 40 76 56 10   **Métro:** George V
Spectacular international cabaret featuring the Bluebell Girls and stunning stage sets. Dinner-dance at 20 hrs, first show 22 hrs, second show at midnight.

Moulin Rouge – Place Blanche, 18e
Tel: 01 46 06 00 19   **Métro:** Blanche
Famed for its association with Toulouse Lautrec. Well known show featuring the 40 Doriss Girls. International revue. Dinner-dance at 20 hrs, first show at 22 hrs, second show at midnight.

Folies-Bergère – 32 Rue Richer, 9e
Tel: 01 44 79 98 98 **Métro:** Cadet/rue Montmartre
In the style of the traditional 19th century music hall – a mixture of variety acts and modern dance routines. One show per evening at 21.15. Open 19 hrs for light pre-show dinner in the prestigious lounge. Also Sun lunch 12.30, show at 15 hrs. Closed Mon.

Crazy Horse Saloon – 12 Avenue George V, 8e
Tel: 01 47 23 32 32   **Métro:** George V
World-famous erotic (but tasteful) show. Performances at 20.30 & 23; Sat at 22.30 & 00.50 hrs.

Opera, ballet and concerts

Tickets for opera and ballet at the Opera House are extremely difficult to obtain. However, you can see the magnificent interior of the Opera House during the day (for a small charge).

An alternative venue is the Opéra Bastille which opened in 1989 to commemorate the bicentennial of the French Revolution. The building offers programmes of dance, opera, concerts and recitals.

Classical music concerts are plentiful, some given in historic churches. See current listings. Also there are other less exalted venues for ballet and dance theatre and opera, especially during the many festivals held in Paris.

Cinema and Theatre

Paris has the widest and most numerous choice of films. Most foreign films are shown in the original. VO (*version originale*) means with French sub-titles. Unless you are a true linguist, avoid films marked VF: this means they are dubbed in French.

Theatre is very varied – but you need fluency in French for full enjoyment.

Chapter Eleven

Children in Paris

Paris is welcoming to children, but Parisians expect children to be better behaved than Americans or British people do. Here are some places and entertainments of special interest to children.

Parks and Playgrounds

Jardin d'Acclimation, 16e.

A 25 acre amusement park in the northern edge of the Bois de Boulogne. Rated as the best children's playground in Paris, it can be reached by miniature train from Porte Maillot (afternoon only). It features a very wide variety of activities and facilities – fairground, adventure playgrounds, animals, miniature farm, rides, house of mirrors, etc. It's a sure bet for pre-teenage children. Open 10.00-18.30 hrs (Sunday to 19.30 hrs).   **Métro:** Porte Maillot/Sablons

Bois de Vincennes

The Bois de Vincennes is a large recreational area with an expanse of woodland, boating lake, museums, and a classical chateau. There is as much for adults to enjoy as in the Bois de Boulogne.

It has the best and most enjoyable zoo in the city. Open daily 9.00-17.30 hrs. Also, on the other (eastern) side of the wood, is the Paris Flower Garden (*Parc Floral*). A miniature train tours the gardens, and there's a children's play area. On summer weekends there are clowns, puppets, etc.

The Musée des Arts Africains et Oceaniens (near the Zoo) should interest older children (8 plus) and adults. Downstairs, too, there is a marvellous tropical aquarium.   **Métro:** Porte Dorée

CHILDREN'S PARIS

Central parks

Many parks in the centre of Paris have children's play and amusement areas – though rather too ordered. Best provided is the **Luxembourg Gardens**, with playground, donkey rides, toy-boat pond, puppets. The **Tuileries garden** has similar facilities.

The gardens of the **Champs-de-Mars** – with the Eiffel Tower alongside – have a children's playground and donkey rides.

Museums

Grévin Museum – Boulevard Montmartre, 9e
The main Grévin waxworks, with some fun ideas and shows. Should be a sure success for children.

Museum of Popular Arts and Traditions – Bois de Boulogne. Has displays for children to operate.

La Villette – See Chapter 5 for play areas. The science museum, the City of Science and Industry, should hold the attention of older children (12 plus). The Géode cinema is likely to amaze one and all.

Toy Shops

Au Nain Bleu – 406-401 Rue Saint-Honoré, 8e
A famous toyshop, worth goggling at, but with luxury prices. Small children will be thrilled by a walk round the store.   **Métro:** Concorde/Madeleine

Ali-Baba – 29 Avenue de Tourville, 7e
Three storeys of toys for all ages.
                                Métro: Ecole-Militaire

Babysitters

Babysitters cost about 50 francs per hour. Your hotel will usually be able to arrange for this. There are several established agencies, including:

Ababa, La Maman en Plus
Tel: 01 43 22 22 11. Includes English speakers.

General Association of Paris Medical Students
Tel: 01 45 86 19 42

Maman Poule   Tel: 01 47 47 78 78

Chapter Twelve

Being City-Wise

Safety and Security

Pickpocketing and bag-snatching are rife in many tourist areas. Keep handbags securely fastened. They should be carried in a way which cannot easily be snatched, such as over the opposite shoulder, across the body.

Never carry wallets, credit cards or money in a pickable pocket. Be specially careful in crowded places such as the Métro. Pickpockets often work in pairs, taking advantage of crowds to jostle and distract their victims while stealing a purse or wallet.

Among the most skilful thieves are groups of gipsy children who roam the main tourist areas of Paris and the Métro. Do not stop if approached by these children and never take out your purse or wallet to give them anything, as it may be snatched.

If something is stolen, report the theft to the nearest police station and obtain an *attestation de vol* (an official declaration of theft for insurance purposes). It will be easier if you are accompanied by someone who speaks French well.

Women on their own can be perfectly comfortable and safe in cafés and on the street. This applies to animated areas which are not clearly disreputable. The Bois de Boulogne is not safe at night. Do not be uneasy if you are stared at during the day. In France it's not rude to admire or look intently at a pretty or interesting face.

Police

Ordinary police are the gendarmes, wearing blue uniforms and *képi* hats. Address a gendarme as: *Monsieur l'agent.*

Emergency Services:

Police: Tel: 17.
Fire: Tel: 18
Ambulance (SAMU): 15

The main Police Station with interpreting service is:
Préfecture de Police, Bureau 1520, Ile de la Cité, 4e.
Open daily 9-17 hrs. Tel: 01 42 77 11 00, ext 4874.

Lost Property

Lost Property Office – address:
Bureau des Objets Trouvés, 36 Rue des Morillons,
15e. Open Mon-Fri 8.30-17.00 hrs (Tuesday and
Thursday until 20 hrs).   **Métro:** Convention

Tipping

Tipping is widely practised. In hotels and restaurants,
15% service is included in the bill. For hotel staff,
see Chapter 2.

● It is common but optional to leave something extra
for the waiter: if you are pleased, say 5-10%.

● For service at the counter in cafés and bars, leave
small change.

● Guides: Museum and tour guides should be tipped:
about 5F for a museum tour; about 10% for an excursion (depending upon length, and numbers of
tourists and so on).

● Taxi Drivers: 10-15%.

● Cloakroom Attendants: about 2F.

● Theatre usherettes: 2F.

Daily Hours

Shops stay open until 18.30 or 19.30 hrs. Some
smaller ones close for lunch. Sunday is a standard
closing day (many food shops open); and also Monday for some neighbourhood shops and food shops.

Paris city centre is far less crowded mid-morning
than in the afternoon. Morning, near opening time, is
the best time to visit museums and the department
stores. Most museums close at 17-18 hrs.

Traffic is most congested in the centre from 16.30
hrs onwards, slowing buses and taxis. The Métro is
packed between 17-19 hrs with rush hour.

Nighthawk hours

Nightlife – clubs, discos and bars – begins late, around 22 or 23 hrs. The Métro finishes about 00.45 hrs. Much nightlife continues until 2 a.m., and a sprinkling of devoted nightlife until dawn.

Public Holidays

Museums and restaurants are mostly open on public holidays. The principal national holidays are: Jan 1; Easter Sunday and Monday; May 1; May 8; Ascension Thursday; Whit Monday; Bastille Day (July 14); Assumption (August 15); All Saints (November 1); Armistice Day (November 11); Christmas Day.

Seasonable Paris

One should visit Paris in every season to enjoy its different aspects.

Winter: best season for nightlife and shows. Very good for shopping (and real bargains in January sales). The period leading up to Christmas is bad for traffic jams, and quite tremendous for shop window displays. Many Parisians leave the city over the Christmas holidays. Museums are less crowded.

Summer: Paris is at its quietest between July 15th and August 25th, when many Parisians are on holiday. Summer is a good time to wander the Partis streets and to discover its buildings. However, August can be sultry.

Spring and Autumn: Paris at its most typical. Spring for a sense of romance, with sparkle in the air; autumn for nostalgia, with the Paris light at its most beautiful.

La Politesse – Manners and Etiquette

The French are considerably more formal than the Americans or British. Manners matter.

On entering a small shop, or acknowledging someone, it is polite to say *Bonjour, Monsieur* or *Bonjour, Madame*. Note that '*Bonjour*' by itself is insufficient. When addressing someone, *Monsieur* and *Madame* may be used without the surname.

Madame is used for an older woman; *Mademoiselle* is used for a young woman or girl.

Say that with a smile and you're off to a good start. Use whenever appropriate the other standard phrases of politeness: *s'il vous plaît* for please, again always followed by *Monsieur* or *Madame*; *excusez-moi* etc.

Don't hesitate to shake hands, briskly and firmly. It is common practice when meeting someone or saying good-bye. Try to use whatever French you can to express your pleasure and regard.

You can dress informally, except for top class restaurants, when ties and suits are expected; in cabaret restaurants (where some people will be wearing evening dress) and for private clubs, not conservatively but appropriately.

You should dress respectfully before entering churches (but a head covering is not necessary).

Language

You should acquire at least some few phrases of French, both for your own needs and for la *politesse*.

The main difficulty for someone with limited French is more in pronunciation than in vocabulary. Try to get help, and practice with pronunciation at any opportunity – from friends, couriers, perhaps your children at school. There are excellent introductory programmes on radio and TV (enquire to the BBC).

There are some characteristic French sounds which once you have got them, will very greatly ease your way in speaking French. Some people advocate that the way to acquire the trick of imitating French sounds is to mimic a strong French accent whilst speaking English. Try this out with anyone who will play.

It is worth getting a simple pocket French phrase book if your French is non-existent or very slight.

Chapter Thirteen

Sunday in Paris

There is plenty happening in Paris on a Sunday but if you should find yourself at a loose end, here are a few suggestions:

Excursions

A variety of excursions are available in Paris on a Sunday. Please check your tour rep for details.

Shops and Markets

Certain shops on the Rue de Rivoli, Champs Elysées and at Les Halles are open on Sundays.

The Marché aux Puces (flea market), Marché aux Oiseaux (bird market) and many other markets are open on Sundays. See 'Shopping' chapter for details. 'Bouquinistes', the small picture and book stalls along the Seine embankments, are often open on Sundays and provide interesting browsing.

Museums and Galleries

A number of museums and galleries are either half price or free on Sundays. Worth buying is a publication called 'l'Officiel des Spectacles' available from newsagents (cost: 2F). Look up 'Musées' – 'Dim gratuit' means free on Sundays or 'Demi-tariff le dim' is half price. This also lists opening hours.

Eating and Drinking

You can of course eat and drink all day in Paris but two Sunday specials are:

Bertillon Ice Creams: these famous ice creams can be enjoyed at Bertillon's, Rue St Louis en L'lle.
Métro: Pont Marie

Tea at Angélinas, 226 Rue de Rivoli – the place to be seen having afternoon tea on Sunday!

Tel: 01 42 60 82 00

Church Services – Anglican

St Georges Church - 7 Rue Auguste-Vacquerie, 16e
Main Sunday service 8.30 and 10.30 hrs.
Tel: 01 47 20 22 51   **Métro:** George V/Kléber

British Embassy Church (St Michael's) – 5 Rue d'Anguesseau, 8e. Main Sunday services 10.30, 11.45, 18.30 hrs.   Tel: 01 47 42 70 88
Métro: Concorde/Madeleine

Church Services – Catholic

You could of course take the opportunity of attending a service in any of the French churches in Paris. These are mainly Catholic, but of course the services are open to all denominations.

Notre Dame Cathedral – Sunday services are held in the Cathedral at 10.00, 11.30 (Mass), 12.30, 18.30, and 20.30 hrs. There is an organ recital every Sunday at 19.45 hrs.
Midweek services at 8, 9 and 12 hrs. Sat 08.30.
Tel: 01 43 26 07 39   **Métro:** Cité

Sacré-Coeur, Montmartre - Sunday services at 7, 8, 9, 10 & 11 hrs.   **Métro:** Abbesses/Anvers

Parks and Gardens

A good solution if the weather's fine and you'd like a little exercise, space and air! See Chapter 6 – Sights and Places to See.

Cinema

Many films in Paris are shown in their original language. 'L'Officiel des Spectacles' or 'Pariscope' (available from newsagents, 3F) are good guides (and good for your French!). Most films you will recognise by their titles or by the actors. The letters VO (*version originelle*) in brackets after the cinema name means that the film is in its original language.

Chapter Fourteen

At Your Service

14.1 Money & Currency Exchange

French currency

The unit of French currency is the franc (usually written F or f). The franc is divided into 100 centimes.

The exchange rate between the franc and the pound sterling and US dollars has ranged very approximately around 8 francs to £1, or 5 francs to the dollar - shifting according to the strength or weakness of the respective currencies.

Check the exchange rate more precisely at the time of your trip.

The following French currency denominations are in circulation:

Coins: 5, 10 and 20 centimes. All copper coloured.
    50 centimes (half franc – silver coloured).
    1, 2 and 5 francs (silver coloured).
    10 francs (either bronze or bronze and silver).
    Notes: 20, 50, 100, 200, and 500 francs.

Amounts in francs and centimes are written as follows:
15.25F or 15F25 – denoting 15 francs 25 centimes.

What to take with you

It pays to change sterling for French francs before you leave Britain and take francs with you. In any case you should have a supply of French francs to tide you over the first day of arrival. That applies even more strongly if you arrive at the weekend or latish in the evening.

Changing Money

You can change money and cheques at banks, exchange bureaux (Bureaux de Change) and larger hotels. You will be required to produce your passport for all transactions except when changing cash. Commission rates vary and can be high in the case of hotels. Generally, banks deduct a flat sum as commission, making it uneconomic to change small sums of money.

Travellers cheques are a safe way of carrying money but may be more difficult to change over a weekend.

Eurocheques can usually be cashed for francs at French banks which display the Eurocheque symbol. Your cheques must be presented with a Eurocheque card (a special card for use abroad, obtainable from your bank in advance) and passport. Production of a normal cheque card, even with a Eurocheque symbol displayed in the corner, will no longer be accepted.

N.B. If you do use your Eurocheque card, the maximum amount you can cash in any one day is 1,200 francs. If you use your Eurocheque card to cash a cheque in Paris on your last day abroad, you will not be allowed to do so the same day in the U.K., because of the £50 limit.

Banks

Normal opening hours: 9.00-16.30 hrs, Monday to Friday. Banks close at 12 noon on the eve of national holidays. Smaller branches close for lunch between 12 and 14 hrs.

British Banks

Barclays
157 Bvd St-Germain (6e)   Tel: 01 42 22 28 63
6 Rond Point des Champs Elysées (8e)
                                 Tel: 01 44 95 13 80
32 Avenue George V (8e)   Tel: 01 53 67 82 20
21 Rue Fbg. St Honoré (8e)   Tel: 01 45 63 53 22
Open 09.00-16.30 hrs Monday-Friday.

Lloyds
15 Avenue d'Iéna   Tel: 01 44 43 42 41
Open 09.00-16.00 hrs., Monday-Friday.

Exchange Bureaux and Banks Open Outside Normal Banking Hours

Charles de Gaulle Airport – 6-23 hrs daily.

Exchange bureaux are open every day at the following railway stations:

Gare du Nord (6.30-22.00 hrs).
Gare de Lyon (6.30-23.00 hrs).
Gare de l'Est, Gare St Lazare, Gare d'Austerlitz (all 7.00-21.00 hrs, except Sunday).
Gare Montparnasse (9.00-19.00 hrs).

The exchange bureaux at railway stations are a last resort, as they are usually crowded and irksome. It is worth making sure that you do not run short of francs and need currency exchange facilities at the weekend or out of normal banking hours.

Credit Cards

American Express, Diners Club and Visa are accepted in many shops and restaurants in Paris; Access less widely. Cash is obtainable at banks with automatic card machines, which can recognise your pin number.

To change money on Access you must go to the Crédit Agricole at either of the following addresses:

14 Rue de la Boétie, (8e)   Tel: 01 42 65 00 32
Open 9.30-13.30, 14.45-17.30 hrs., Monday-Friday.
                              Métro: St Augustin
16 bis Bd de Sebastopol, (4e)   Tel: 01 42 78 03 54
Open 9.15-17.00 hrs Mon to Sat.   **Métro:** Châtelet

To change money on Visa:-

Crédit Commercial de France
115 Champs Elysées, (8e)
Métro: Charles de Gaulle-Etoile
Open 8.30-20.00 hrs daily.

In both cases, you will probably be required to produce your passport.

14.2 Post and Telephone

The postal and telephone service is known as PTT (pronounced 'pay tay tay'). Post Office hours are 8-19 hrs Mon-Fri; 9-12 hrs Sat.

Stamps (*timbres-poste*) are obtainable at Post Offices (*bureaux de poste*) and at tobacconists and hotels.

The central Post Office is at 52 Rue du Louvre, 1er (**Métro**: Louvre). It is open 24 hours every day for telephone and telegraph; until 19 hrs for other services.

Telephones

You can place calls from any post office. You pay after the call.

You can phone through the switchboard of your hotel, and will be charged at a higher rate.

You can use a payphone. With the popularity of card-phones, it's often difficult to find a phone operated by coins. Especially if you're phoning home, it's worth buying a phonecard or Télécarte (40.60F or 97.50F for 50 or 120 units), available as for stamps. This lets you use many more public telephones in working order.

International Calls

To make a call abroad, note the code number of the country you want (e.g. USA 1, UK 44). Here is how to proceed when calling UK from payphones:

● Lift receiver
● If the phone is coin operated, insert at least 10F.
● Dial 00, then 44 (the international code for the UK) plus the appropriate UK local area code, less the initial 0. Thus, to call Bristol (dialling code 01272) 12345, dial 00-44-1272-12345.
● Should you hear any recorded announcements in French, this probably means either that you have dialled the wrong number or that the lines are engaged.
● A flashing black and white disc at the top left of the coinbox will indicate that more coins are needed to continue your call.

Calls within Paris

Note that all French phone numbers have been converted to ten digits since October 1996. All 8-digit Paris numbers are now preceded by 01.

Calls to other parts of France

Depending on the Province you are phoning, add 02, 03, 04 or 05 in front of the former eight-digit number.

Reverse Charge Calls (known as PCV)

Dial 100 and ask operator for the number.

Note that there are cheaper evening rates and very much cheaper rates at night and on Sundays.

14.3 Medical Matters

You should take out personal travel insurance to cover any medical expenses. This will also cover theft, loss of luggage, etc.

Visitors from other EC countries are entitled to medical treatment under the French social security system. But, to qualify, you must have the necessary documentation with you.

If you are a British citizen, you need to obtain Form E111 from the Department of Health and Social Security. Allow over a month to apply for this form and receive it.

In France, you pay for medical treatment at the time and about 70 per cent of the cost is refunded by the French social security.

On a short visit to France, it is more convenient to use a private insurance policy than Form E111 and social security. Should you consult a doctor, keep the receipt and any prescription to claim a refund from your insurance.

Doctors

The fee for a straightforward visit to a doctor is about 100F. If you need an English-speaking doctor for important or urgent problems, contact:

SOS Médecins (24 hours; house visits) – 87 Boulevard Port-Royal, 13e.   **RER:** Port Royal
Tel: 01 43 37 77 77 or 01 47 07 77 77.

AT YOUR SERVICE

Dentists

For urgent dental treatment:

SOS Dentistes (24 hours; house visits) – (Same address as SOS Médecins).   Tel: 01 43 37 51 00
The American Hospital also has a dental clinic open 24 hours a day: see under Hospitals below.

Pharmacists or Chemists

Pharmacies will help with minor ailments and first aid. Some English-speaking pharmacies are:

Pharmacie Anglaise des Champs-Elysées – 62 Avenue des Champs-Elysées.   Tel: 01 43 59 22 52 Open: 8.30-22.30 hrs, Mon-Sat. **Métro:** George V
British-American Pharmacy – 1 Rue Auber, 9e Open: 8.30-22.00 hrs, Mon-Sat.   **Métro:** Opéra
Pharmacie des Arts – 106 Bd Montparnasse, 14e Open: 8-24 hrs, Mon-Sat; 9-13 hrs Sun and Public holidays. Tel: 01 43 35 44 88.   **Métro:** Vavin

Hospitals

Hospitals with English-speaking staff are:

American Hospital – 63 Bd Victor-Hugo, Neuilly Outpatients: 9-18 hrs; Emergency service 24 hours daily. Tel: 01 46 41 25 25. **Métro:** Pont Levallois
Franco-British Hospital – 3 Rue Barbès, Levallois-Perret. Tel: 01 46 39 22 22. **Métro:** Anatole-France

14.4 Embassies and Consulates

UK Embassy: 35 Rue du Faubourg St-Honoré, 8e
Tel: 01 42 66 91 42
British Consulate: 16 Rue d'Anjou, 8e
Tel: 01 44 51 31 00
USA: 2 Rue Saint-Florentin, 1er
Tel: 01 42 96 14 88
Australia: 4 Rue Jean-Ray, 15e
Tel: 01 40 59 33 00
Canada: 35 Av Montaigne, 8e Tel: 01 44 43 29 00
Ireland: 12 Av Foch, 16e   Tel: 01 45 00 20 87
New Zealand: 7 Rue Léonard-de-Vinci, 16e
Tel: 01 45 00 24 11

Chapter Fifteen

A Pick of Paris

Here is a varied selection of special recommendations that might well appeal even to those who know Paris well. Each entry is the best we know, inside a reasonable price limit.

Everything here is exceptional; and also everything here is truly representative of Paris. At the end of your Paris city break, why not compile your own listing?

Best Bus Route

Bus No 24. A superb route for great monuments and the river Seine. Starting from Gare St Lazare, it goes round the Place de la Madeleine (luxury food shops), into Place de la Concorde, along the Seine by the Tuileries gardens, and past the Louvre.

There's a view across the river of fine buildings – the Mint (called Hôtel des Monnaies) and the Institut de France (home of the immortal Académie Francaise). The bus crosses the river on the Pont Neuf to the Ile de la Cité, the island on which Notre Dame stands, past the law courts (Palais de Justice), and crosses over the Petit Pont to the Left Bank.

It goes east along part of the Boulevard St-Germain and then Quai St Bernard beside the Seine. If you want to return on the 24 bus, get off on the Quai St Bernard by the Jardin des Plantes (long before the terminus). Explore these gardens if you wish. By Métro, the Gare d'Austerlitz is handy.

On the return journey, the 24 bus passes along the Seine's left bank, with a splendid view of Notre Dame, and passing near the corner of Musée d'Orsay. It crosses the river by Pont Royale and returns to St Lazare via Concorde and rue Royale.

Best View

La Samaritaine Department Store, 1er

Rue de la Monnaie (between Pont Neuf and rue de Rivoli). Best 360-degree view of Paris.

The store occupies four separate grand buildings. Enter Magasin 2 (Store 2) and take elevator to 9th floor, where you can have a drink in the café. Go upstairs to 10th floor where the roof terrace offers a matchless panorama of Paris and stunning views over the River Seine.

Five Other Great Views

Eiffel Tower, 7e   See Chapter 5.

The highest panorama: from its summit level platform you can see 50 miles on a clear day. If it's cloudy you may see Paris better from the second stage level. The lift costs 56F to the top deck.

Arc de Triomphe, 8e   See Chapter 5.

There is a uniquely satisfying view from the top of the Arc de Triomphe, with twelve great avenues radiating from Place Charles de Gaulle, and views to Montmartre and the Pantheon.

Tour Montparnasse (Montparnasse Tower), 14e.

This is the only skyscraper in central Paris. The 56th floor has a viewing gallery (with spoken commentary in English), bar and restaurant. The lift shoots you up in 38 seconds. You can reach the open roof terrace, upstairs two floors higher. The view makes an interesting variation to that from the similar height of the Eiffel Tower; and it's also more pleasant.   **Métro:** Montparnasse Bienvenue

Open: 9.30-23.30 hrs, Summer; 10.00-22.30 hrs, Winter. Cost: 42F.

Notre Dame, 4e   See Chapter 5.

From one of the fastest lifts in Europe at Montparnasse we go to worn and winding stairs of the cathedral. A strenuous climb rewards you with a closer look at the gargoyles and a thrilling view of Paris.

The South Tower offers the better view. In this tower hangs the great 13-ton bell immortalised by

Victor Hugo and known to millions through Charles Laughton's acting as the hunchback Quasimodo. It is 252 steps to the Grande Galerie and another 90 to the South Tower. Entrance to Towers on north of cathedral in Rue Cloître-Notre-Dame, daily except Tue, cost 28F (reduced 18F). **Métro:** Cité

Montmartre, 18e   **Métro:** Anvers/Abbesses
The hill of Montmartre offers some of the most attractive and romantic views of Paris, especially spellbinding at dawn or dusk. Look from the steps of the Sacré-Coeur (see chapter five), or for a larger panorama climb to the dome from which you can see across virtually the whole city.

The most interesting and the most satisfying view is not necessarily the highest. The expanse of the highest views is at the cost of detail and form. For sheer beauty, the views of Paris from the quays and bridges around the Ile Saint-Louis and the Ile de la Cité are among the greatest in Paris.

Note in particular the views from the Pont de la Tournelle and from the Quai d'Orléans on the Ile Saint-Louis. Also, behind the Quai de Montebello on the Left Bank, the remarkable view from Square Viviani, one of the most appealing and inspiring in Paris.

For two superb views of monumental Paris, note the terrace of the Palais de Chaillot and the Alexandre III bridge (see Chapter 6).

Most Picturesque Square

Place des Vosges, 4e
The most beautiful square in Paris, and the oldest (built 1612). An unspoiled, authentic Parisian antique, in the Marais district.
       Métro: St-Paul/Chemin-Vert

Most Magnificent Square

Place de la Concorde, 8e   See Chapter 5.
Possibly the finest square in the world, in the most glorious and dazzling setting. The best viewpoint is from the centre, preferably when the traffic is relatively sparse, such as early Sunday morning.

Most Fashionable Square

Place des Victoires, 2e

This circular square (built in the 17th century) has recently become a hub of new fashion. Modish boutiques and restaurants have blossomed in its noble mansions. **Métro:** Bourse

Most Opulent Square

Place Vendôme, 1er

A very grand square set apart by wealth. Here are great jewellers, perfumiers, art dealers, bankers, and the Ritz Hotel. **Métro:** Tuileries/Opéra

Finest Lingerie

Nina Ricci – 39 Avenue Montaigne, 8e

Here is some of the world's most beautiful lingerie; also other feminine accoutrements and an impeccably Parisian dress collection. (If you venture beyond the ground floor with its fabulous prices and exclusive air, there is a bargain basement with big discounts.)

If the ambiance is too daunting, there is a superb lingerie department at Galeries Lafayette, the department store in the Boulevard Haussmann.

Best Dresses and High Fashion

Fashion and Textile Museum (Musée de la Mode et du Textile) – in the Louvre

Opened 1986, surprisingly this is the first collection in Paris to be devoted to fashion. The museum has over 20,000 costumes from 17th century to the fashions of today. More details Chapter 6.

Best Jazz

New Morning – 7-9 Rue des Petites-Ecuries, 10e

The best jazz club and, together with Ronnie Scott's, the best in Europe. Comfortable and spacious with good sound and visibility and the prime venue for visiting American musicians of every jazz style.

Open from 21 hrs. Tel: 01 45 23 51 41.

Métro: Château-d'Eau

Most Elegant Afternoon Tea

The Lancaster Hotel – 7 Rue de Berri, 8e

Delicate cucumber sandwiches, scones and cakes served in lovely surroundings: in the drawing room or in the courtyard in summer. The hotel still retains its original atmosphere of a fine private house.

Métro: George V

Best Old-Fashioned Afternoon Tea

The Tea Caddy – 14 Rue St-Julien-le-Pauvre, 5e

Cinnamon toast, crumpets, scones – it would be difficult to find better in England. Served in a very old house with wood panelling. Refined, but moderate prices. In Latin Quarter, just across the bridge from Notre-Dame. **Métro:** St-Michel

Best Hot Chocolate

Angélina – 226 Rue de Rivoli, 1er

The *chocolat chaud* (hot chocolate) is unsurpassed. Angélina's is the pre-eminent tea salon in Paris. You should not miss eating its Mont Blanc, a concoction of chestnut cream purée and meringue. But the choice in cakes and pastries is boggling.

Métro: Tuileries/Concorde

Best Ice Cream

Berthillon – 31 Rue St-Louis-en-l'Ile, 4e

No better ice cream known, but better service can be had. At Berthillon's you queue for the best. Open Wed-Sun 10-20 hrs, but closed in August at the height of the ice cream season and also during some school holidays. **Métro:** Pont-Marie

If you want to eat Berthillon's ice cream without queueing, go round the corner, also on the Ile Saint Louis, to La Flore en l'Ile, 42 Quai d'Orléans. This sunny tea room also has good views of the Pantheon on the Left Bank, and of Notre Dame.

Best Fast Food

Crêpe Stall, 6e – corner of Place St-André-des-Arts and Place St-Michel.

True sophistication in fast food looked after by

a woman who has been many a year in the crêpe business. A real French service.   **Métro:** St-Michel

The Greatest Food Shop

Fauchon – 26 Place de Madeleine, 8e

The most celebrated food store in the world and the best. A wonderful treat even if you just look. Fauchon could also be nominated for the prize window display. At its perfection in the early morning, this is a visual feast not to be missed.

If you want to buy, the shop is expensive but a treasure house for presents. Across the road is Fauchon's stand-up Café where prices are moderate for superlative home-made cakes etc, and the most excellent coffee or tea. A recognised institution for Parisians, but don't expect courtesies for tourists.

Métro: Madeleine

Best and Most Cheese

Androuet – 41 rue d'Amsterdam, 8e

The foremost Paris temple to cheese. Look with wonder at the variety of cheeses on display, all kept in perfect condition. At noon and 7 p.m. you can have a remarkable 2½-hour course in cheese tasting and cheese lore – but it's all in French. It is also a restaurant where you can have a 4 course meal of cheeses!   **Métro:** Saint-Lazare

Best Fish and Chips

Hamilton's Noted Fish and Chips

51 Rue de Lappe, 11e   **Métro:** Bastille

All the fish and chip essentials generously supplied; take-away or eat in the shop with a good choice of English beer. Open: Mon-Sat 12-14 hrs; 18.00-23.30 hrs; Sunday 18-23 hrs.

Best Children's Slide

Dragon Slide in the Parc de la Villette, 18e

A slide shaped as a dragon, 35 yards long. Children enter at the tail, crawl through the undulating belly, and emerge from the fiery mouth. For park details, see Chap 5.

Métro: Porte de la Villette

Best Park Bench

In the gardens of the Champs-Elysées there is a path named Allée Marcel Proust. Proust, the great novelist, played here. He mentions this bench in his masterpiece, and it is a good place to contemplate the pleasure of being in Paris.

Best Garden Retreat

Musée Rodin, 7e   See Chapter 6.
For a haven, go into the garden of the Rodin Museum near Les Invalides. The repose of the garden is enhanced by the sculptor's works, and the lovely mansion that houses the museum itself.

Best Sunset

Go to the Square du Vert-Galant on the Ile de la Cité. From this little green park on the western tip of the island, watch the sun set on the Pont des Arts.   **Métro:** Pont Neuf